www.osha.gov

Employers are responsible for providing a safe and healthful workplace for their employees. OSHA's role is to assure the safety and health of America's workers by setting and enforcing standards; providing training, outreach, and education; establishing partnerships; and encouraging continual improvement in workplace safety and health.

This publication is in the public domain and may be reproduced, fully or partially, without permission. Source credit is requested, but not required.

This information is available to sensory impaired individuals upon request. Voice phone: (202) 693-1999; teletypewriter (TTY) number: (877) 889-5627.

Fire Service Features
of Buildings and Fire Protection Systems

Occupational Safety and Health Administration
U.S. Department of Labor

OSHA 3256-07N
2006

Acknowledgments

Numerous individuals assisted in the development of this document. OSHA wishes to express its deepest appreciation to the following individuals for their significant contributions to this manual.

Edwin G. Foulke, Jr.
Assistant Secretary

The following persons provided a courtesy technical review:

David M. Banwarth, P.E.
David M. Banwarth Associates, LLC (DMBA)
Samuel S. Dannaway, P.E.,
President and Chief Fire Protection Engineer, S.S. Dannaway and Associates, Inc.
Former Volunteer Firefighter, Prince Georges County, MD.
Ivan J. Humberson, P.E.
Fire Marshal, City of Gaithersburg, MD.
Former Volunteer Firefighter, Prince Georges and Frederick Counties, MD.
Greg Jakubowski, P.E., CSP
Senior Program Safety Specialist, Merck & Co., Inc.
Penn. State Fire Instructor
Captain, Lingohocken Fire Company, Bucks County, PA.
Chris Jelenewicz, P.E.
Engineering Program Manager, Society of Fire Protection Engineers
Past Chief, Chillum-Adelphi Volunteer Fire Dept., MD.
Michael J. Klemenz, P.E.
Davis-Ulmer Sprinkler Company, Inc.
Past Deputy Chief, Liverpool, N.Y. Fire Department
James Lathrop
Vice President, Koffel Associates, Inc.
Deputy Chief, Niantic, CT Fire Department
Eric. N. Mayl, P.E.
Fire Protection Engineer, Koffel Associates, Inc.
Captain (Ret.) D.C. Fire Department
Jim Tidwell
National Director, Fire Service Activities
International Code Council
Executive Deputy Chief (Ret.), Fort Worth Fire Department, TX.

The following persons contributed photographs or diagrams for this manual:

David Banwarth, P.E., Banwarth & Associates
Jeff Cisney, P.E., General Services Administration
Glen Ellman, Freelance Photographer
Michael Eversole, U.S. Secret Service
John Guyton, Prince Georges County Fire Department, MD (retired)

Neal Hobbs, Montgomery County Fire and Rescue, MD.
Ivan J. Humberson, P.E., Fire Marshal, City of Gaithersburg, MD.
Bryan Iannacone, College Park Volunteer Fire Department, MD.
Michael J. Klemenz, P.E., Davis-Ulmer Sprinkler Company, Inc.
Vito Maggiolo, Freelance Photographer
National Fire Protection Association
N.J. Department of Community Affairs, Division of Fire Safety
Rockville, MD Fire Marshal's Office
Rick Schartel
Michael Schwartzberg, Freelance Photographer
Marty Smith, Alarm Tech Solutions
Tempe, AZ Fire Department
Anthony Turiello, Rescue Air Systems, Inc.
Queens Printer of Acts of Parliament, U.K.
Craig Willms, College Park Volunteer Fire Department, MD.
Jeff Woodard, College Park Volunteer Fire Department, MD.

The following persons contributed their professional expertise and assistance:

Anthony Catroppo, Alarm Tech Solutions
Mike Eversole, U.S. Secret Service
Beth Forbes, Washington Suburban Sanitary Commission
Nicholas S. Havrilla, Jr., University of Maryland
Heather Heath, N.Y. Empire Chapter, Society of Fire Protection Engineers
Mark Lentocha, Chesapeake Chapter, Society of Fire Protection Engineers
Dallas Lipp, Montgomery County Fire and Rescue, MD.
Jeffery P. McBride, P.E., EBL Engineers, LLC
Mary McCormack, Fire Department Safety Officer's Association
Kevin McNamara, College Park Volunteer Fire Department, MD.
Tommy Nguyen, College Park Volunteer Fire Department, MD.
Michael Ramey, Operations Manager, Alarm Tech Solutions
Kevin Riley, Phoenix Fire Department, AZ.
Thomas W. Shand
Tom Slane, College Park Volunteer Fire Department, MD.
Scott Stookey, Phoenix Fire Department, AZ.
Anthony Turiello, Rescue Air Systems, Inc.
Steve Welsh, Fire Protection Engineer

OSHA
Occupational Safety and
Health Administration

Contents

OSHA
Occupational Safety and
Health Administration

Chapter 1
Introduction

PURPOSE

The purpose of this manual is to increase the safety of building occupants and emergency responders by streamlining fire service interaction with building features and fire protection systems. The information in this manual will assist designers of buildings and fire protection systems to better understand the needs of the fire service when they are called upon to operate in or near the built environment (figure 1.1). To put this another way, architects and engineers create workplaces for firefighters. Designs can be tailored to better meet operational needs, thereby reducing the time it takes to mitigate an incident.

The guidance in this manual is expected to decrease the injuries to responding and operating fire service personnel. When an incident can be mitigated faster, there is less time for the hazardous situation to grow in proportion. With less potential exposure, employees occupying buildings will be afforded greater protection from fire incidents. Employee occupants as well as fire service employees will realize the benefits of this manual in terms of safe working conditions as intended by the *Occupational Safety and Health Act of 1970.*

The codes and standards governing buildings and fire protection systems are well understood by designers. However, many portions of these codes and standards allow design variations or contain only general performance language. The resulting flexibility permits the selection of different design options. Some of these options may facilitate fire service operations better than others.

The particular needs and requirements of the fire service are typically not known thoroughly by persons not associated with these operations. This manual discusses how the fire service interacts with different building features and it suggests methods for streamlining such interaction. To provide the most effective protection, fire service personnel should be considered as users of building features and fire protection systems. While far less frequent than mechanical events or other failures, fire can cause greater destruction in terms of property loss, disruption of operations, injury, and death.

Designers routinely consider the needs and comfort of building occupants when arranging a building's layout and systems. Within the framework of codes and standards, design options may

(Fig. 1.1) Commercial building fire at night with multiple exposures.

be exercised to benefit a particular owner, tenant, or user. For example, a building code would typically dictate the minimum number of lavatories and water fountains. However, the location, distribution, and types of such facilities are left to the designer in consultation with the client.

The application of fire protection features in buildings is similar. For instance, a fire code may require the installation of a fire department connection for a sprinkler system or an annunciator for a fire alarm system. However, there may be little or no guidance as to the location, position, features, or marking of such devices. This manual provides this type of guidance to designers. However, specific local requirements or preferences may differ. Input should always be obtained from local code officials and the fire service organization, the "client" in this case.

SCOPE

This manual is to be used voluntarily, as a companion to mandatory and advisory provisions in building codes, life safety codes, fire codes, safety regulations, and installation standards for fire protection systems. The material contained in this document focuses on ways that building and fire protection system designers can contribute to the efficiency of fire suppression operations.

This material is applicable to all fire service organizations, including fire brigades and fire departments. Many of the considerations in the following chapters will also help during responses for other emergencies, such as hazardous materials releases, emergency medical care, non-fire rescues, and terrorist events.

Users of this manual must understand its limitations. It is directed to designers of buildings and fire protection systems to help them build on existing codes and standards to assist the fire service. For example, the topic of emergency radio communications can be extensive; however, its treatment here is limited to the equipment in buildings that can support radio communications. Likewise, there are entire standards and books written about sprinkler, standpipe, and fire alarm design. However, this manual covers only portions of those systems with which the fire service interacts and suggests design details that will help streamline or support fire service operations.

A FIRE SERVICE PRIMER

This section will give those outside the fire service a basic understanding of how the fire service operates during an emergency. It will also familiarize them with the varying capabilities and organizations involved in fire fighting.

Fire service organizations can be classified as career, volunteer, or a combination of both. Career staff members are paid for their work, while volunteer members are unpaid. Combination organizations have both career and volunteer staff. Career organizations typically serve the larger, more urban or industrial settings, although many smaller cities or towns will have a full or partial career staff. Volunteer organizations are usually found in more suburban or rural settings, although some serve densely populated areas and have very high emergency response rates.

Another way to categorize fire departments is by whether fire stations are staffed with personnel ready to respond. Most career organizations have personnel who remain in the station while on duty. However, "call firefighters" are paid on a per-response or hourly basis and do not remain in their station awaiting emergency calls. Most volunteers respond from home or work when they are alerted to an emergency. On the other hand, there are organizations that have volunteer personnel staffing their stations on shifts or even living in the stations.

Another fire service organization is the industrial fire brigade. This is an organized group of employees specifically trained to provide fire suppression, and perhaps related emergency activities, for a specific employer. Members may be dedicated full time to emergency operations, or emergency response may be a part-time, collateral duty.

(Fig. 1.2) A view from above of both a pumper (top) and an aerial apparatus (bottom), in this case a platform type of aerial.

A typical emergency begins with the discovery and reporting of an incident. The time span of this phase can vary greatly, and the fire service has no control over this. After the report is received, the information is processed and the appropriate units are alerted. Those firefighters not staffing the station (whether volunteer, paid on-call, or collateral duty fire brigade members) must travel to the station. Firefighters then don their protective equipment, board the vehicles, and the response phase begins. In some organizations or scenarios, members not staffing the station may go directly to the incident scene.

OSHA
Occupational Safety and
Health Administration

(Fig. 1.3) During initial operation at this structure, the first arriving engine crew is already using a fire lane, a fire hydrant, the fire department connection, and the key box. Interior operation will soon involve the alarm system, stairways, standpipe system, and other building features.

The fire service response to a structure fire would normally involve a number of different units. Fire department vehicles are called apparatus; one is sometimes referred to as a "piece" of apparatus. They come in a wide variety of forms for specialized uses; however, the basic types are pumper and aerial apparatus (Figure 1.2).

A pumper apparatus normally carries hose, a pump, and a small water tank. Together with its personnel, this is called an engine company. Their main responsibility is to deliver water to the fire. Initially, the engine company may operate using the water available in their tank; however, any incidents other than small exterior fires will typically require that a continuous water supply be established. This is done via hose lines carrying water from a source of supply (fire hydrant, lake, pond, temporary basin) to the on-board pump, which then boosts the pressure to hose lines or other devices attacking the fire.

An aerial apparatus is typically equipped with a long aerial ladder or elevating platform on top, an assortment of ground ladders, and many power and hand tools. Together with its personnel, this is often called a truck (or ladder) company. They are responsible for all support functions, including forcible entry, search, rescue, laddering, and ventilation. If aerial apparatus is not available, these truck company functions must be performed by another unit.

There is also an apparatus called a "quint." Each of these vehicles is equipped as both a pumper and an aerial apparatus to perform either function. If provided with adequate staffing, and positioned properly at an incident, quints can perform both functions.

Upon arrival at an incident, firefighters must handle many tasks. Standard operating procedures should enable firefighters to quickly assess the situation, and initially arriving units to go into operation (Figure 1.3). Rescuing of occupants is the first priority, followed by confining and extinguishing the fire. In some cases, firefighters must stop the fire before proceeding with rescues.

Incident command begins with the rapid gathering of information by the first arriving officer. This is called "size-up." Incident command expands as additional units and chief officers arrive. Commanders must base strategies on the limited information available at any given time regarding the fire, the building, and the occupants. As they receive additional information, commanders should revise their strategies. As needed, they can call for additional resources. Units from another jurisdiction or district that respond are referred to as "mutual aid" units.

As the fire incident is brought under control, salvage, overhaul, and investigation activities take place. These activities, although dangerous and important, are less time-sensitive. As a result, they are less of a consideration for building and fire protection system designers.

FIRE SERVICE CHALLENGES

Fire service operations take place in stressful, time-sensitive environments (Figure 1.4). Delaying operations, even slightly, especially during the critical initial phase when the first arriving resources are committed, can adversely affect subsequent operations and the outcome. Delays caused by poorly located fire hydrants, confusing alarm information, ineffective communication systems, or inaccessible valves will have a ripple effect on the other portions of the operation. During these delays, the fire will be growing exponentially.

Members of the fire service perform their functions during all times of the day or night, in any weather conditions, and frequently in unfamiliar environments. Their work environment is dangerous, mentally stressful, and physically exhausting. Decisions must often be made without an ideal amount of information, due to the many unknowns on the fireground (such as what is on fire, how much is burning, where the fire is spreading, and where the occupants are located).

These factors stack the deck against the safety of firefighters. Even simplifying the firefighters' job in small ways will increase the level of safety for them, and thereby for building occupants. Design features that save time or personnel can make a great difference. Any feature that provides additional information regarding the fire, the building, or the occupants, as well as any method to speed the delivery of this information also helps.

Pre-incident plans (often called "preplans") are documents prepared by fire departments to assist in emergency operations in specific facilities. They should contain the location of, and information about, the fire protection features discussed in this manual. Preplans are usually prepared and maintained by the unit that normally responds first, or is "first due," to a particular facility. One could argue that some of the considerations in this manual are not necessary if the fire department prepares thorough preplans. However, the best pre-incident planning cannot overcome situations where the first due unit is committed on another response, out of position, or out of service. Nor can it foresee changes in personnel. It is simply unrealistic to count on all responding personnel to be aware of the pre-incident plan.

Pre-incident planning makes sense but it will always have limitations. Fire departments and firefighters that are more familiar with features of

(Fig. 1.4) Firefighters arriving at a high-rise fire. During this operation, firefighters will interact with most of the features discussed in this manual. To successfully mitigate an incident of this nature, firefighters must make many decisions rapidly, and carry out various operations simultaneously. Time saved due to design with the fire service in mind will translate into increased firefighter and occupant safety.

buildings in their response area are better prepared to deal with fires and other emergencies. Designers can assist in pre-incident planning by providing copies of building and system plans (paper or electronic) to the fire service after first seeking permission from the building owner.

National Fire Protection Association (NFPA) statistics show a steady decline of fire-related deaths in the U.S. during the 1990s. During that same decade, however, the number of firefighter fatalities has remained relatively steady. The National Fallen Firefighters Foundation has developed a list of safety initiatives to reduce firefighter line-of-duty deaths and is playing a lead role in their implementation.

MANUAL ORGANIZATION AND USE

Each chapter of this manual includes a narrative describing the specific building feature and how the fire department interacts with it. Boxes, entitled "Considerations," highlight specific items that a designer should consider for each topic. Photos and diagrams illustrate both good and bad examples of concepts and recommendations.

Occupational Safety and Health Administration

Although this manual contains generic considerations, designers should seek and follow the advice of the fire service organization serving each project they work on. In some cases, the fire department will have statutory authority to take part in the plan review, permit process, and inspections of these facilities or to approve some features of the building or site. In any case, it is wise to also include the fire service at an early stage in the design process, when changes are easier and less costly.

There are many ways for the fire protection community to disseminate or incorporate the information in this manual. Simply handing it out to designers is a great start. Developing a handout based on this document that is specific to a particular jurisdiction is another good strategy. The recommendations can also serve as a basis for local code amendments which carry the force of law.

Many of the recommendations in this manual cost nothing to implement. They simply provide direction in cases where the model codes or consensus standards allow options. Designers can implement these recommendations directly, in consultation with the fire department. Other recommendations in this manual may carry costs, depending on the particular codes adopted in a given jurisdiction. In such cases, those who would be affected by these costs should be consulted.

Codes and standards typically include a clause that permits the code official to allow alternatives to strict compliance, as long as the prescribed level of safety is not diminished. In some cases, a higher level of safety for firefighters can be achieved through this process. For example, a voluntary radio repeater system may provide more protection (and may also be less costly to install) than a code-required firefighter communication system. Equivalent alternatives should be documented along with justification.

This manual may also serve as a resource for those interested in improving codes and standards for building or fire protection system design. While current codes in the U.S. provide for firefighter safety, much more remains to be accomplished. For instance, building codes in the U.K. have specific fire service provisions, such as dedicated, protected fire stairs and elevators. Streamlining and simplifying fire service operations should be considered an integral part of the overall fire safety framework for the built environment.

TERMINOLOGY

The terminology used in this manual is as generic as possible, just as it is in the standards of the National Fire Protection Association and the International Code Council. Many variations in terms will be encountered in different areas of the U.S. or in other countries. For example, this manual uses the term "aerial apparatus" to describe a fire service vehicle with a long, aerial ladder. Yet, in this country alone, other terms used to describe the same vehicle include: "truck," "ladder," "aerial," "ladder truck," "tower," or "tower ladder." Or, in some cases, the same terms could be used to describe a particular aerial fire apparatus. Similarly, in some areas the term "truck" refers only to aerial apparatus, while in other areas this term could also include pumper apparatus.

In another example of potentially confusing terminology, fire apparatus drivers in some areas of the country are referred to as "engineers." Consider the situation of an architect speaking to a fire officer in an area where this terminology is used. You can easily see how the fire officer could use the term "engineer" to mean a driver, while the architect interprets the term as a building design engineer.

The editions of the codes and standards referenced in this manual are not included. The information and requirements referenced in this manual are from the latest editions available during the manual's development in 2004. Subsequent revisions to these codes and standards may change the sections or the requirements referenced. The editions adopted by local or state laws in a given jurisdiction may vary.

GLOSSARY OF ACRONYMS AND TERMS

AHJ (Authority Having Jurisdiction): the entity legally designated to enforce a code or standard.

Apparatus: fire service vehicle.

Apparatus, aerial: apparatus that carries ladders and tools.

Apparatus, pumper: apparatus that carries hose, a pump, and a water tank.

Apparatus, quint: apparatus that contains aerial and pumper equipment.

Code Official: a fire code official, building code official, or authority having jurisdiction.

Code Official, Building: person legally designated to enforce a building code.

Code Official, Fire: person legally designated to enforce a fire code.

Engine company: pumper apparatus and personnel.

First due unit: engine company or truck company designated to respond first to an incident at a given location.

Hose lay, straight (or forward): an engine company evolution (task) to lay hose from a water source to an incident scene or another unit.

Hose lay, reverse: an engine company evolution (task) to lay hose from an incident scene or another unit to a water source.

Hose line, preconnected: a hose of fixed length with a nozzle attached and connected to a discharge outlet on a pumper.

IBC: International Building Code.

IFC: International Fire Code.

Ladder company: aerial apparatus and personnel.

NFPA: National Fire Protection Association.

NFPA 1: Uniform Fire Code.

NFPA 101: Life Safety Code.

NFPA 241: Standard for Safeguarding Construction, Alteration, and Demolition Operations.

NFPA 1141: Standard for Fire Protection in Planned Building Groups.

NFPA 5000: Building Construction and Safety Code.

Pre-incident plan: document containing information on a specific facility to facilitate emergency operations.

Truck company: aerial apparatus and personnel.

Occupational Safety and
Health Administration

Chapter 2
Building and Site Design

GENERAL

The faster the fire service can respond, enter, locate the incident, and safely operate in a building, the sooner they can mitigate an incident in a safe manner for themselves as well as occupants. This chapter contains guidance on this topic for both building site layout and interior design features. Those preparing design documents such as site plans, civil plans, foundation plans, and architectural layouts would typically use this information. Building designers desiring to locate fire protection systems features should consult the appropriate chapters of this manual for further guidance.

FIRE APPARATUS ACCESS

Properly positioning fire apparatus can be critical at a fire scene. In particular, placing aerial apparatus is critical for positioning of the aerial ladder or elevating platform, which is mounted on top of these vehicles (Figure 2.1). Pumper apparatus also need to get close enough to the building to facilitate hose line use. The location of other specialized apparatus, or small vehicles, such as chief's cars or ambulances, should only be of particular concern to the designer of unusual facilities. For instance, a sports arena may need to be designed for entry of ambulances but not fire apparatus.

Many structures are situated on public streets that provide fire fighting access. Others, which are set back from public streets, have private fire apparatus access lanes or "fire lanes," for short. These enable fire apparatus to approach the building and operate effectively (Figure 2.2). Fire lanes can be dedicated to fire service use, or can serve ordinary vehicular traffic as well.

There are many considerations for both public roads and fire lanes: clear width, clear height, length, turn radius, arrangement, distance from the building, and paving materials. In all cases, the most stringent practicable dimensions should be considered for design, since future apparatus purchases or mutual aid apparatus from other jurisdictions may exceed the specifications required in a given jurisdiction at any given time.

Extent of Access

Minimum building access for fire apparatus is a function of the access road reaching to within a certain distance of all portions of the building's first

(Fig. 2.1) Good aerial apparatus access at an apartment fire. This fire lane is wide enough to allow passing even when aerial outriggers are extended, and it is located a proper distance from the building to facilitate aerial operations.

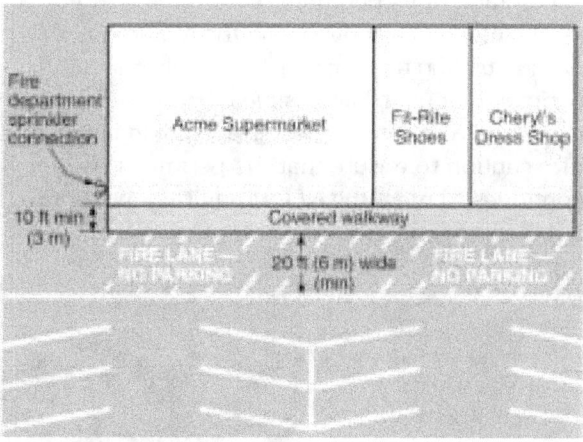

(Fig. 2.2) Fire lane dimensions, reprinted with permission from NFPA 2003 Uniform Fire Code Handbook, © 2003, National Fire Protection Association, Quincy, MA.

floor exterior walls. This limit in NFPA 1 and the IFC is 150 feet for buildings without a complete sprinkler system. For fully sprinklered buildings, NFPA 1 permits this distance to be increased to 450 feet; the IFC leaves this decision up to the discretion of the code official. Further, NFPA 1 requires that the road extend to within 50 feet of an exterior door providing interior access.

The distance from the building to a road or fire lane is sometimes referred to as "setback distance." NFPA 1141 has additional guidelines for access locations versus building location, with variations depending upon building size, height, sprinkler protection, and separation from other buildings.

Perimeter Access
The options available for attacking a fire increase as more of a building's perimeter becomes accessible to fire apparatus (Figure 2.3). A concept, known as "frontage increase," appears in the IBC and NFPA 5000. If a structure has more than a certain percentage of its perimeter accessible to fire apparatus, these codes allow the maximum size of the building to be increased. Ideally, the full perimeter would be accessible.

During renovations, designers should use particular caution to ensure that the perimeter access continues to meet the NFPA requirements of fire

and building codes. The original building site may have been based on a frontage increase. Changing the amount of perimeter access can result in non-compliant building size.

Number of Fire Lanes
A single access route is a basic requirement in both NFPA 1 and the IFC. However, both codes allow the code official or AHJ to require additional access routes due to various factors that could inhibit access (such as terrain, climate, or vehicle congestion). NFPA 1141 requires two access routes for buildings over two stories or 30 feet in height. Multiple fire lanes should be as far removed from one another as practicable.

Turnarounds
Long, dead-end fire lanes or roads should provide a means for fire apparatus to turn around. Both NFPA 1 and the IFC require turnaround space for dead-ends that are more than 150 feet long. There are a number of configurations that facilitate turning maneuvers. These include, "T-turn," "Y-turn," and round cul-de-sac style arrangements (Figures 2.4 and 2.5 for NFPA diagrams). NFPA 1141 requires a 120-foot turnaround at the end of dead-ends more than 300 feet long. Turnaround diagrams also can be found in Appendix D of the IFC.

(Fig. 2.3) A combination of two public roads and two private fire lanes provides full perimeter access to this building.

OSHA
Occupational Safety and
Health Administration

Clear Width

The basic clear width requirement for apparatus access in the IFC and NFPA 1 is 20 feet. NFPA 1141 calls for one-way fire lanes that are 16 feet wide; however, this applies to roads that do not abut buildings. A clear width of 20 feet will allow most aerial apparatus to extend the outriggers necessary to support the aerial ladder or elevating platform while in operation (Figures 1.2 and 2.1). However, some recently manufactured aerial apparatus require 24 feet of clear width for outrigger extension.

Lanes wide enough for apparatus to pass one another will facilitate developing and expanding operations. NFPA 1141 contains a 24-foot clear width requirement for two-way fire lanes. Appendix D of the IBC calls for a 26-foot clear width at fire hydrant locations, extending for a distance of 20 feet in both directions, as well as a 26-foot width in the vicinity of buildings that are 30 feet or more in height (for aerial operations). NFPA 1141 also contains guidance on access in parking lots.

Rolled or rounded curbs adjacent to properly designed sidewalks can effectively increase access width. These allow apparatus to easily negotiate curbs.

Height

The basic requirement for clear height of fire lanes in the IFC, NFPA 1 and NFPA 1141 is 13 feet 6 inches. Some modern aerial apparatus may require 14 feet of clearance. Potential for accumulation of snow and ice should be factored into height requirements. The NFPA 1 handbook recommends at least 14 feet in colder climates. Newer aerial apparatus may also require additional height. Finally, avoid overhead wires or other obstructions when determining fire lane locations.

(Fig. 2.4) Fire apparatus "Y-" and "T-turnarounds." Reprinted with permission from NFPA 2003 Uniform Fire Code Handbook, © 2003, National Fire Protection Association, Quincy, MA.

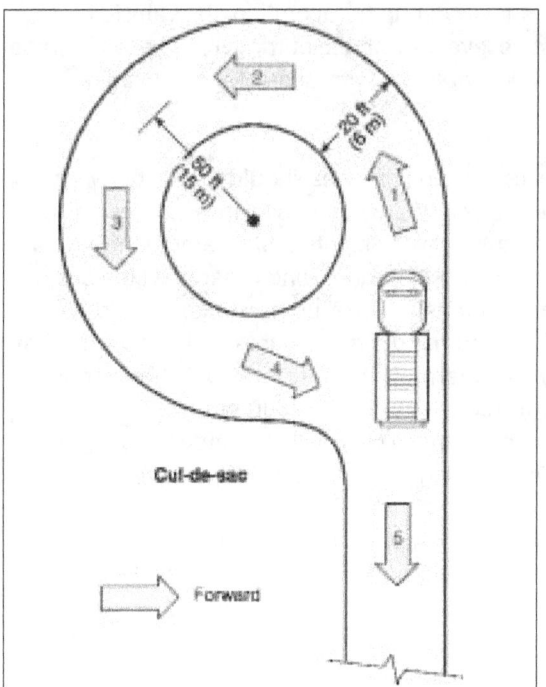

(Fig. 2.5) Fire apparatus cul-de-sac turnaround. Reprinted with permission from NFPA 2003 Uniform Fire Code Handbook, © 2003, National Fire Protection Association, Quincy, MA.

Building Proximity

In areas with aerial apparatus that may respond to an emergency, the road or fire lane should be positioned at a distance from the building that will accommodate aerial ladder operation. Access too close or too far from the building will limit aerial ladder use. Where a fire lane is parallel to a building that is more than 30 feet high, Appendix D of the IFC calls for the near edge of the lane to be between 15 and 30 feet away from the building.

Turn Radius

The IFC and NFPA 1 leave turn radius requirements to the code official and AHJ. However, NFPA 1141 requires a minimum inside turn radius of 25 feet and a minimum outside radius for turns of 50 feet. The cul-de-sac depicted in Figure 2.5 shows an effective inside turn radius of 40 feet. Further, NFPA 1141 requires 2-foot curb cuts on either side of a fire lane where it connects to a road.

Grade

NFPA 1 sets a maximum grade (slope) of 5 percent for fire lanes. NFPA 1141 specifies a 10 percent maximum, as well as a 0.5 percent minimum to prevent pooling of water. However, some manufacturers have lower limits for specific apparatus. When aerial apparatus is set up for operation, the vehicle body must be leveled with the outriggers. The least grade possible would allow for the most rapid setup.

Loads

All access roads or lanes should be built to withstand the loads presented by modern, heavy fire apparatus as well as potential weather conditions. Paved surfaces, bridges, and other elevated surfaces (such as piers or boardwalks) should be designed to handle the weight of all apparatus that may use them. The IFC Appendix D has a load design requirement of 75,000 pounds. U.S. Department of Transportation standards dictate requirements for both load and frequency. The IFC references the Standard Specification for Highway Bridges from the American Association of State Highway Transportation Officials (AASHTO).

(Fig. 2.6) Paver blocks were chosen instead of paving for this access road. The aesthetic benefits are minimal, and the road cannot be plowed effectively.

(Fig. 2.7) The same paver block access lane as shown in Figure 2.6, but covered with snow. Access is blocked by a mound of snow plowed from the adjacent parking lot.

Materials

All-weather paved access is the best surface. Some jurisdictions permit the use of paver blocks or subsurface construction for fire lanes (Figure 2.6). These permit an area to be partially or fully landscaped, while being strong enough to allow fire apparatus to negotiate the area. However, these materials do have inherent limitations. Unless their perimeter is clearly marked, it is easy to drive off the edge. Also, in regions subject to snow accumulation, areas with paver blocks and subsurface construction cannot be plowed effectively (Figure 2.7).

(Fig. 2.8) Manual gates cause inherent delays because personnel must dismount to unlock them or cut through chains. However, they can also help keep the fire access lane clear by preventing vehicle parking.

(Fig. 2.9) The delays caused by electronic gates can be minimized by providing the fire department with access cards or remote access controls.

Gates, Barricades and Security Measures

Security concerns may impact fire service access. Gates (manual, electric, or radio controlled), bollards, pop-up barricades, and other perimeter controls can delay fire service operations. On the other hand, these access control measures can assist in keeping vehicular traffic away from fire lanes (Figures 2.8 through 2.10). During the design phase of a project, careful coordination between those responsible for security and fire protection can help resolve both concerns. In addition, proper gate size, location, and swing can facilitate fire service access. Wooden bollards are designed with cuts

near their bases to allow access when apparatus bump them and break them. However, this results in delays while they are broken and cleared from the path of the apparatus, and may also cause damage.

Speed Control Measures

Speed bumps or humps can impact fire apparatus access. Due to their suspension, these vehicles must come to a nearly complete stop to pass over these bumps, delaying arrival to a fire scene. Some special speed bump designs allow for fire apparatus to straddle bumps, while passenger vehicles cannot do so. Dips should also be avoided so that long wheel-base vehicles do not hit bottom and damage undercarriage components and overhanging equipment.

Marking

Fire lane signage is important, both for the public and enforcement officials (Figure 2.8). Examples include signs, curb painting, or curb stenciling. A jurisdiction's requirements must be followed exactly to ensure that no-parking provisions are legally enforceable. Speed bumps should be conspicuously painted, and signs indicating their location should be posted in climates subject to accumulation of snow and ice. Load limits should be posted conspicuously on both ends of bridges or elevated surfaces.

(Fig. 2.10) Pop-up barricades such as these are appearing more frequently due to security concerns. Unless security forces are constantly present to operate them, however, the fire department should be provided with a means to do so.

Considerations – Fire Apparatus Access

- Extent of Access: Within 150 feet of the farthest exterior point; can be farther in sprinklered buildings.
- Perimeter Access: As many sides of the building and as much of the perimeter as possible; take advantage of frontage increases.
- Number of Fire Lanes: More than one when dictated by code official or AHJ.
- Turnarounds: Provided for on all dead-ends more than 150 feet long.
- Clear Width (excluding parking): Minimum 20 feet; preferably, 24 feet to allow passing and 26 feet in the vicinity of fire hydrants or points of aerial access.
- Clear Height: Minimum 13 feet 6 inches; higher where subject to accumulations of snow and ice.
- Obstructions: Avoid overhead wires and other obstructions.
- Proximity to Buildings for Aerial Operations: If parallel to buildings more than 30 feet high, locate near edge 15–30 feet away.
- Turn Radius: Minimum 25 feet inside and 50 feet outside.
- Curb Cut: If provided, extend 2 feet beyond on each side of intersecting fire lane.
- Grade (slope): Maximum 5 percent; least grade possible for aerial operation areas.
- Load: Access routes, both on grade and elevated, designed for the largest possible apparatus load.
- Materials: Design access routes for all-weather use.
- Security Measures: To minimize delays, specify that keys, electronic access cards, or remote access controls are provided to the fire department.
- Barricades: Use non-destructive gates or posts rather than breakaway bollards.
- Gate Size: At least 2 feet wider than fire lanes.
- Gate Location: At least 30 feet from public right-of-way.
- Gate Swing: Away from direction of fire apparatus travel.
- Speed Bumps: Avoid them, or design them for fire apparatus.
- Signage: Provide for no-parking areas, and for load limits.
- Special Apparatus: May require more stringent criteria than above.

PREMISES IDENTIFICATION

The fire service must be able to rapidly identify and locate a specific building. Address numbers should be placed on the building facing the street or road on which the building is addressed. If the building entry faces a different street, both the street name and the number should be on the address sign.

Numbers should be large enough to read from the street or road. If this is not possible due to the location of the building or due to obstructions, additional signs should be provided (Figure 2.11). The IFC specifies that address numbers be a minimum of 4 inches high. Some jurisdictions have a higher minimum height requirement, especially for commercial properties. The number should be in Arabic numerals rather than spelled out (for example, "120" instead of "One Hundred Twenty").

Buildings set back in groups that share common entrances can make quickly locating a specific building and the shortest route to it difficult. On such sites, additional signs with directional arrows and/or diagrams of the buildings and access layout should be posted (Figures 2.12 and 2.13).

Whenever possible, signs should be illuminated. In areas subject to snow accumulation, signs should be positioned above anticipated accumulations.

See the section Firefighter Access on page 21 for signage to assist the fire service in identifying portions of a building, or interior layouts.

(Fig. 2.11) Supplemental address sign at the entrance serving this building set far back from the road.

OSHA
Occupational Safety and
Health Administration

(Fig. 2.12) Directional address sign at the entrance of a property.

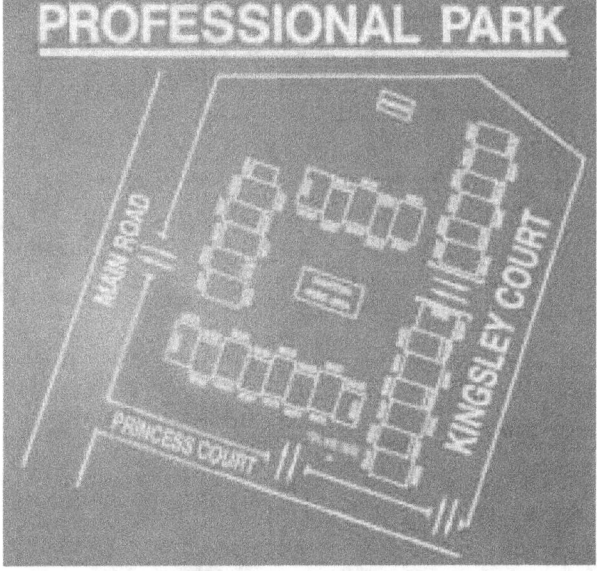

(Fig. 2.13) Diagrammatic sign showing an entire complex of buildings and their address(es). The addition of fire hydrant locations (and any other fire protection features) would assist responding firefighters.

Considerations – Premises Identification

- Location: Addresses should be on each building.
- Numeral size: At least 4 inches high for single family homes, and preferably 6 inches high for all other properties; larger if necessary to be visible from the street.
- Numerals: Addresses (numbers) should be in Arabic numerals.
- Color: Addresses should be in a color that contrasts with the background.
- Provide street name with the address number for entrances facing other streets.
- Provide additional address signs at entrances to the property when the building address is not legible from the public street.
- Common entrances: Provide directional or diagrammatic signs for groups of buildings sharing common entrances; include locations of fire hydrants, fire department connections, and fire alarm annunciator panels.

FIRE HYDRANTS

Optimal positioning, spacing, location, and marking of fire hydrants can aid the fire service during emergency operations. Public fire hydrants are often under the purview of a local water authority, many of whom use American Water Works Association (AWWA) standards for fire flow and other criteria. The building design team is often responsible for hydrants and water supply systems on privately owned property sites. Both the IFC and NFPA 1 include appendices that give criteria for fire flow, and fire hydrant location and distribution. Other criteria can be found in NFPA 24, Standard for the Installation of Private Fire Service Mains and their Appurtenances.

(Fig. 2.14)   This hydrant should not have been located where it is likely to be blocked. Loading docks, by nature, will likely have vehicles parked. This is an example of building a potential deficiency into a facility. The truck could prevent use of the large pumper connection or cause the base to be kinked when used. Note the yellow bollards which protect the hydrant from vehicle collision.

Features

Typically, hydrants have a large suction hose connection ($4\frac{1}{2}$ inches is a common size) called a "pumper outlet" or a "steamer" connection. Plus, they normally have two, $2\frac{1}{2}$ inch hose connections. Both wet-barrel type hydrants and the dry-barrel types used in areas subject to freezing have these features. Dry hydrants (those connected to a static source such as a tank, well, or pond) often have only a large connection or pumper outlet. Criteria for dry hydrants can be found in NFPA 1142, Standard for Water Supplies for Suburban and Rural Firefighting.

Hose can be connected directly to a fire hydrant only if the connections match those needed by the area fire service. This includes type (threaded or quick-connect), thread style and size of connection. If the connections do not match, adapters (if available) will slow response.

Position

Optimal location and positioning of hydrants facilitates rapid connection of hose lines and devices. Considerations for designers include height, orientation, distance from the curb, and distance from surrounding obstructions (Figure 2.14). A clear distance is essential around the hydrant to enable a hydrant wrench to be swung 360 degrees (see Figure 2.16b) on any operating nut or cap nut. If the nearby obstruction is a plant or bush, consider its potential growth when planning for hydrant placement.

(Fig. 2.15) Here is a pumper connected to a hydrant by its front-mounted suction hose. The pumper end of the hose has a swivel to facilitate reaching hydrants on either side.

OSHA
**Occupational Safety and
Health Administration**

(Fig. 2.16a) Pumper stopping to initiate a forward hose lay from a hydrant.

(Fig. 2.16b) The same pumper completing the straight lay towards the fire scene, and a firefighter preparing to operate the hydrant after the hose is safely layed out.

(Fig. 2.16c) Pumper performing a reverse hose lay from a fire scene (to feed the monitor nozzle shown) towards a hydrant.

Spacing

Maximum distance between hydrants differs greatly, depending on various local standards. IFC and NFPA 1 both include tables within appendices that enable a designer to find the required fire flow for any given building, and then select the corresponding hydrant spacing. Where apparatus may approach from different directions, hydrants should be placed primarily at intersections. If additional hydrants are needed to comply with local spacing requirements, they should be spaced along blocks at regular intervals.

Location

Pumpers may utilize hydrants in different ways. If the fire is close enough, a pumper can be positioned at a hydrant and use a large-diameter suction hose (Figure 2.15). Pumpers in urban and suburban areas with hydrants are generally equipped with large-diameter suction hoses connected to an intake on the pumper's front bumper, rear step, or side. This suction hose may be as short as 15 feet. In many urban areas, however, pumpers carry longer suction hoses in order to reach hydrants on the opposite side of a single line of parallel parked cars.

If a fire is not close to a particular hydrant, a pumper may have to lay one or more hose lines between the hydrant and the fire. If a pumper lays a supply hose line from a hydrant towards the building with the fire emergency, this is called a "straight" or "forward" hose lay (Figures 2.16a and 2.16b). The opposite (laying supply hose from a building on fire to a hydrant farther down the

street) is called a "reverse lay" (Figure 2.16c). Many fire departments use one or the other of these options as their standard procedure. Designers should take this into account when locating hydrants. For instance, hydrants at the end of dead-end streets will not facilitate straight hose lays.

Hydrants that are too close to a particular building are less likely to be used due to potential fire exposure or collapse. Locating hydrants at least 40 feet away from protected buildings is recommended. If this is not possible, consider locations with blank walls, no windows or doors, and where structural collapse is unlikely (such as building corners). A rule of thumb for collapse zone size is twice the distance of the building's height. This is not a consideration in urban areas, where a multitude of hydrants are available for any given location.

Marking

A number of methods are used to enable firefighters to rapidly identify hydrant locations. The color used for hydrants should contrast as much as possible with the predominating surroundings. Some localities place reflective tape around the hydrant body. Other jurisdictions mount reflectors (usually blue) in the roadway in front of each hydrant; however, in cold weather climates these reflectors are often obstructed by snow.

The best way to identify hydrants in areas subject to snowy weather is a locator pole which is visible above the highest expected snowfall. These are

(Fig. 2.17) One example of a hydrant locator pole with a reflective flag.

reflective or contrasting in color, and some have a flag, sign, or reflector mounted on top (Figure 2.17). These poles should be flexible enough to return to their upright position if someone tampers with them, or rigid enough to prevent this type of tampering. Some jurisdictions or sites go so far as mounting a light (usually red or blue) above the hydrants.

A color coding system may indicate flow capability of hydrants. One such system is contained in NFPA 291, Recommended Practice for Fire Flow Testing and Marking of Hydrants.

During construction or demolition, fire hydrants may be out of service. Designers should specify that inoperative hydrants be covered or marked during their projects, so that firefighters will not waste time attempting to use them.

Considerations – Fire Hydrants
- Position: Orient the pumper outlet toward the access lane or street.
- Height: Center of lowest outlet should be 18 inches above grade.
- Location: Within 5 feet of an access lane or street; preferably with no intervening parking.
- Protection: Provide bollards if there is no curb between the road surface and the hydrant; locate at least 3 feet from the hydrant.
- Obstructions: Locate 3 feet from any surrounding obstructions.
- Consider fire department approach directions and hose-laying procedures when locating hydrants.
- Avoid locations likely to be blocked, such as loading docks.
- Position hydrants at least 40 feet from buildings they serve.
- Specify a hydrant marking system; in cold climates, use distinctive poles.
- Where possible, color code hydrants to indicate flow.
- Specify that inoperative hydrants be covered or marked.

FIREFIGHTER ACCESS

Once firefighters have arrived and positioned their apparatus, they must go to work. Some factors affecting their efficiency include: the distance and terrain between the apparatus access and the building; how easily they can enter the building; the building's interior layout and vertical access (stairs/elevators/roof access); and, how quickly firefighters can locate fire protection features and utilities. The designer can make a positive impact in all of these areas.

Site access

Firefighters must hand carry all equipment beyond the point where apparatus access ends. Increased distance translates into additional time and effort to set up ladders, hose lines, and other equipment. If the area is easy to negotiate by foot, firefighters can move more quickly. The IFC and NFPA 1 contain requirements for access to building openings, such as approved walkways that lead from the apparatus access points to the entry doors.

Fire department pumpers carry hose lines for attacking fires. These are usually smaller in diameter than the hose lines used to supply water to the pumper from a water source. Many pumpers have one or more hose loads of a fixed length connected into a pump discharge. These are "pre-connected" hose lines, often called simply "preconnects." Firefighters deploy them rapidly for quick fire attack. However, their useful range is limited by their length, which is generally between 100 and 400 feet. Designers planning unusual designs for their buildings or working with unusual sites should coordinate with the local fire department regarding hose line access unless a standpipe system is provided in the building.

Buildings under construction or renovation pose their own particular concerns to the fire service. Code provisions can be found in the IFC Chapter 14, IBC Chapter 33, NFPA 5000 Chapter 14, and NFPA 241. Designers should consider the accessibility of fire department connections, fire hydrants, and entry points. Some locations may be more likely to be obstructed by construction storage, truck unloading, cranes, phasing of the construction, and security fences. Designers should consider specifying these locations and the location of temporary and permanent fire protection equipment to avoid conflicts (Figures 5.14 and 5.15).

Key Boxes and Entry Doors

If firefighters need to conduct interior fire suppression operations, they must enter the building at one or more points. The fire service has an array of tools to force entry into buildings. However, forcing entry takes extra time and usually damages the building.

Key boxes (also called "access boxes" or "lock boxes") are small lockable vaults mounted outside building entrances (Figure 2.18). They are opened with a master key held by the fire department. Inside the box are the building's keys. Some jurisdictions require key boxes; others give building owners the option of installing them, or risking the need for firefighters to force entry into their buildings along with any resulting damage. Code officials enforcing the IFC and NFPA 1 may require key boxes. When key boxes are optional, designers may want to educate owners on their benefits.

(Fig. 2.18) Key box adjacent to fire command center. These boxes are often provided at main building entry doors. Note the fire department connection on the left.

(Fig. 2.19) Apartment locator. This door does not access apartments whose windows flank it.

(Fig. 2.20) Rear doors of a shopping center labeled for rapid access: utility room, fire protection equipment room, and individual tenant space.

First arriving firefighters will often base their point of entry on which windows have fire or smoke venting from them. In most cases, entrances that serve any particular window will be readily apparent from the outside. If it is not obvious which door to enter to reach which area, signs or diagrams should be provided outside each entrance door indicating portions of the building accessible from the corresponding door (Figure 2.19).

In multi-tenant buildings, such as shopping centers and malls, tenants usually have rear exit doors that firefighters may access. Often these doors look alike, making it hard to correlate a given door with a particular tenant. Labeling rear doors on the outside with the tenant's name, address number and/or suite number, using lettering at least six inches high with a ½ inch stroke (thickness of lines in each letter) prevents this problem (Figure 2.20).

Any door that appears to be functional from the outside, but is unusable for any reason, should have a sign reading "THIS DOOR BLOCKED." The lettering should be at least six inches high with a ½ inch stroke. If these doors are properly marked, firefighters will not waste time trying to gain entry through them.

Interior Access

Large, unusual, or complex buildings present a challenge to maneuvering and locating specific areas. Directional signs with room/tenant numbers, and graphic directories of tenant/agency layout can assist the public (Figure 2.21). The same diagrams may assist firefighters if they include: stairway and elevator identifiers, fire hose valve locations, fire alarm control panel location, fire alarm annunciator location, fire pump location and other fire protection features. Diagrams should also contain features to assist unfamiliar users with orientation, such as road names or a compass point.

Detailed floor plans showing building layout and fire protection systems can assist the fire service. In buildings with fire command centers, a good location for these plans is in this command center. In other buildings, these plans may be locked inside the fire alarm annunciator panel.

**Occupational Safety and
Health Administration**

Equipment and Utility Identification

A routine function in any advanced fire suppression operation is to control (usually shut down) utilities. Making it easy to locate and identify utilities will speed firefighters' progress. Electric, gas, and other fuel controls should be located either in dedicated rooms with exterior marked entrances, or at exterior locations away from openings such as windows or doors (Figure 2.20).

NFPA 170, Standard for Symbols for Use by the Fire Service, contains symbols for marking gas and electric shut-offs. Air handling equipment should also be prominently marked, especially if located out of sight. The fire service may need to quickly access rooms containing the following equipment: water service, control valves, fire pumps, electric service, switchgear, generators, fans and other mechanical equipment. Lettering for this signage should be at least six inches high with a ½ inch stroke (thickness of lines in each letter), unless the standard symbols are used.

Marking of fire protection system devices within buildings is discussed further in the chapters on fire alarm systems, sprinkler systems, standpipe systems, and fire department connections.

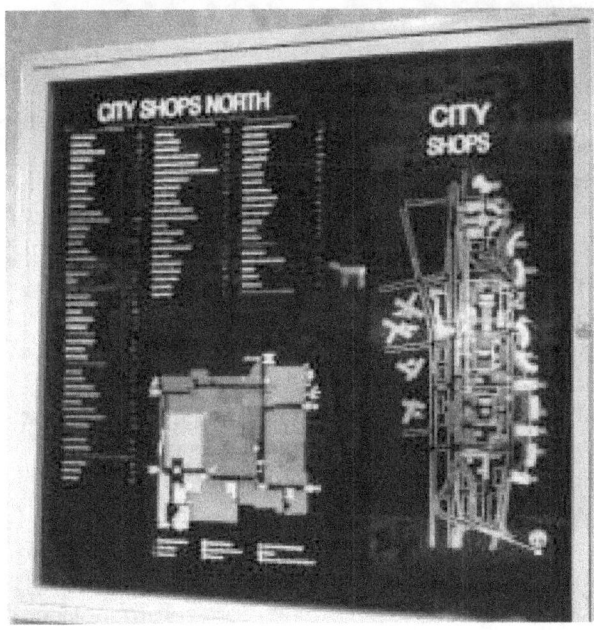

(2.21) Shopping complex diagram with views of the overall complex as well as the interior tenant diagram of the building in which the diagram is located.

Elevators

The use of elevators during fire incidents is very controversial. Elevators are not usually used for occupant evacuation. One exception is trained operators evacuating occupants with special needs. They should, however, be designed for fire service use. The elevator standard widely referenced in building and fire codes is ANSI A17.1, Safety Code for Elevators and Escalators. It details the two phases of emergency operation.

Phase 1 of elevator emergency operation consists of a recall system that automatically sends elevators to a "designated" primary level. This occurs upon activation of a manual recall switch at the designated level or upon activation of smoke detectors in the elevator lobbies, hoistways, or machine rooms. If a detector is activated on the designated primary level, the elevator cars go to an alternate floor level. In either case, the elevators are rendered unavailable to building occupants. They remain at the recall level with doors open, so the fire service can quickly determine that they are clear of occupants and then use them in a manual control mode.

The designated recall level usually is the ground or entry level. This will facilitate rapid fire department access. For buildings with entrances on multiple levels, designers should consult the fire department about the entrance firefighters intend to use initially. The fire department may also prefer to coordinate the designated recall level with the location of the fire alarm annunciator, fire control room, and/or the fire department connection.

Phase 2 emergency operation permits the fire service to use the elevators under their manual control. Phase 2 operation overrides all automatic controls, including the Phase 1 recall.

Solid-state elevator control equipment operates correctly only if maintained within a certain temperature range. NFPA 101, NFPA 5000, and the IBC require independent ventilation in machine rooms containing solid-state equipment that controls elevators traveling over certain distances. Whenever such elevators receive emergency power, their corresponding machine room ventilation would also receive emergency power. These features help maintain at least one elevator operational throughout fire suppression operations.

Currently, ANSI A17.1 requires an automatic power shutdown feature for elevators that have fire sprinklers located in their machine rooms and, under certain conditions, in hoistways. Shutdown occurs upon or prior to the discharge of water, usually when heat detectors mounted next to each sprinkler head are activated. These heat detectors have both a lower temperature rating and a higher sensitivity (a lower response time index) than the sprinkler. However, to minimize the chance that firefighters will be trapped by a power shutdown, the temperature rating of the heat detector should be as high as feasible. Another shutdown method involves water flow detectors; however, these detectors cannot employ a time delay, so designers seldom choose this method. Note that in many cases NFPA 13, Standard for the Installation of Sprinkler Systems, permits sprinklers to be omitted from these areas.

The National Fire Alarm Code, NFPA 72, requires that smoke detectors in either the elevator hoistway or the elevator machine rooms trigger separate and distinct visible annunciation at both the fire alarm control unit and the fire alarm annunciator. This alarm notifies firefighters that the elevators are no longer safe to use, and it also provides some warning time prior to the shutdown feature that is required with sprinkler protection. In addition, ANSI A17.1 requires a warning light in elevator cabs to flash when an elevator problem is imminent.

Stairs

NFPA 1, NFPA 101, NFPA 5000, the IBC, and the IFC all require that identification signage be provided inside stairwells at every level (Figure 2.22). These standards all require stairwell signs in buildings over a certain height, but the height thresholds vary. Signage should show the stair identifier, floor level, terminus of the top and bottom, roof accessibility, discharge level, and direction to exit discharge. On floors that require upward travel to reach the exit, a directional indicator should also be provided. It is important that these signs be located 5 feet above the floor and be visible with the stair door open or closed. In hotels or other buildings with room or suite numbers, the signs should also include the room or suite numbers most directly accessed by each stair on every level, (i.e., second floor of stairway 3 has direct access to rooms 202 through 256). The latter signage would be extremely important where certain stairways provide no access to some sections of the building.

Buildings more than 3 stories in height above grade should have roof access. The IBC and IFC require this, except for buildings with steeply-pitched roofs (with a more than 4:12 slope).

As stated above, the IFC, the IBC, NFPA 5000, and NFPA 241 contain special construction/demolition requirements. One stairway should be completed as construction advances. Conversely, as demolition progresses, one stairway should be maintained. These standards also address lighting and fire rating of the enclosure.

Stair Capacity

Building and fire codes typically require that stairs accommodate exiting occupants. Fire service personnel who may use the stairs are not factored into exit capacity calculations. In situations where occupants are still exiting and firefighters are using the same stairs to enter the building ("counter-flow"), the evacuation may take longer.

Furthermore, in most cases, stairway capacity is designed based on the floor with the highest occupant load. Typically, stairs are not widened as one travels in the direction of egress unless the stairs converge from both above and below. This approach assumes that people will evacuate in a phased manner, beginning with the floor(s) closest to the fire origin. In an immediate general evacuation, or when people from other areas self-evacuate, the increased load will slow evacuation.

Both of these bottlenecks will be made worse as the height of the building increases. Furthermore, total evacuation is becoming more commonplace due to concerns about terrorism.

(Fig. 2.22) Stairway ID sign.

OSHA
Occupational Safety and
Health Administration

An effective solution to the counter-flow issue is a dedicated firefighting stairway. Codes in the United Kingdom contain specifications for such firefighting stairs, elevators, and intervening lobbies in buildings of a certain height (Figure 2.23). Current U.S. codes do not require dedicated stairways or elevators. The disadvantages of dedicated firefighting stairways include: cost, space, and the effort needed to keep them clear and in operating order.

A solution to egress delays caused by either counter-flow or total evacuation is to provide additional exit capacity by means of additional stairs or widened stairs. Cost and space are also disadvantages of this solution.

These issues currently remain unresolved in the code community; however, a designer may encounter these issues on projects for large, high-security, or high-profile facilities. Further guidance on the movement of people in buildings can be found in the Society of Fire Protection Engineers' publication, Human Behavior in Fire.

Diagram 52 **Components of a firefighting shaft**

firefighting lobby

self-closing fire doors

firefighting stairs

firefighting lift in lift shaft

Notes:
1 Outlets from a fire main should be located in the firefighting lobby.
2 A firefighting lift is required if the building has a floor more than 18m above, or more than 10m below, fire service vehicle access level.
3 This Diagram is only to illustrate the basic components and is not meant to represent the only acceptable layout. Ventilation measures have not been shown (refer to BS 5588: Part 5 Code of practice for firefighting stairs and lifts).

(Fig. 2.23) Dedicated firefighting stairway/elevator tower. © Crown Copyright 2000 Queen's Printer of Acts of Parliament.

Considerations - Firefighter Access
- Consider firefighter foot access in site design.
- Avoid using areas that are likely to be obstructed (i.e., shipping and receiving areas).
- Label blocked doors with exterior signage.
- Coordinate temporary construction storage and loading areas with access points and fire protection features.
- Provide key boxes when required; recommend their use in other areas.
- Locate key boxes as recommended by the particular fire department.
- Include fire protection features on building directories.
- Provide signs or diagrams at limited access entrances.
- Identify rooms containing utility shutoffs and fire protection equipment.
- Coordinate elevator recall level with fire service operating procedures.
- Design elevator shutdown feature to minimize the chance of trapping firefighters.
- Provide identification signs at each level of every stairway.
- Extend stairs up or down with construction or demolition; consider the need for lighting and rated enclosure.
- Where total evacuation of a large building is likely, consider additional egress capacity.
- Where firefighter counter-flow is expected, consider additional egress capacity or dedicated firefighting stairs.

(Fig. 2.24) Building with wood truss construction. The adjacent finished building shows no indication from the exterior that wood trusses were used in its construction.

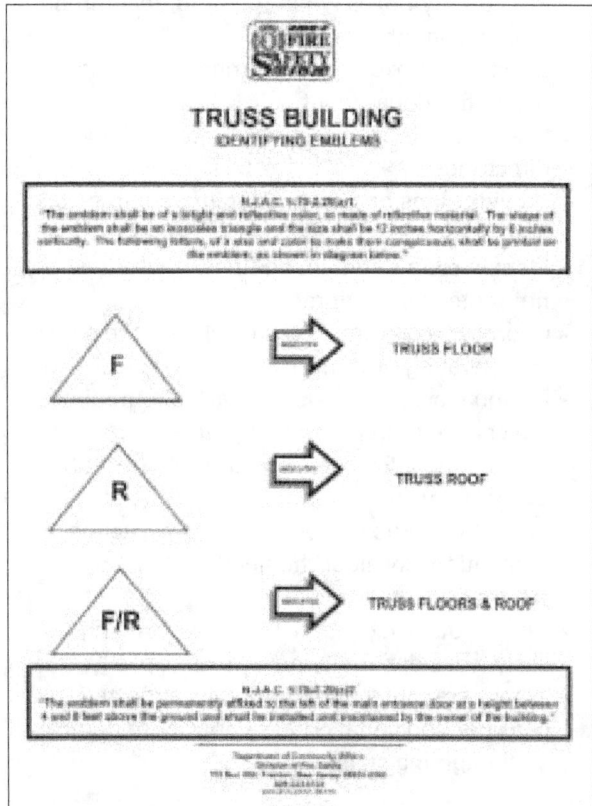

(Fig. 2.25) New Jersey truss building identification emblems.

HAZARDS TO THE FIRE SERVICE

During a fire, any building may become inherently unsafe for occupants and fire service personnel. However, some building construction features present unique or unexpected hazards. This section discusses these hazards.

Lightweight Construction

Trusses are widely used in construction to span wide areas without the need for vertical supports, reducing both material and construction costs (Figure 2.24). Under ordinary conditions, trusses work well and building codes have permitted this type of construction for many years. However, trusses often fail suddenly and totally during fires. Both wood and metal trusses are made of interdependent members which all fail if one member fails. Adjacent trusses, in their weakened state, are then unable to carry the additional load and these also fail in quick succession. It is impossible for crews operating at a fire to predict the time or extent of a collapse since they cannot see how many trusses are affected, which components, and to what extent.

Wood trusses have less mass than solid lumber, which greatly reduces the "extra" wood compared to solid joists that burn through more slowly and provide indications to firefighters of an impending collapse. The higher surface area-to-volume ratio of trusses compared to joists allows trusses to burn more quickly. In addition, the metal gusset plates that hold wood truss components together may fail quickly as fire consumes the wood in which the gusset teeth are shallowly embedded.

Many firefighters have been killed in collapses attributed to trusses, particularly wooden ones, since the 1970s. Incident commanders and/or safety officers typically consider the presence of trusses in their fireground risk analysis. Marking these buildings that include trusses makes this information immediately available to firefighters. The State of New Jersey requires this as a direct result of five firefighters losing their lives in Hackensack in 1988 (Figure 2.25).

Another component used to maximize construction efficiency is the wooden I-beam. Similar to trusses, I-beams eliminate extra wood, thereby providing less warning prior to failure under fire conditions. However, they lack the metal gusset connection plates that appear to be at the root of many wood truss failures.

OSHA
**Occupational Safety and
Health Administration**

Wherever these lightweight construction techniques are used, serious consideration should be given to providing sprinkler protection throughout the building, if not already required. Sprinkler protection of combustible concealed spaces is an important feature for firefighter safety.

Further discussion about lightweight construction can be found in "Building Construction for the Fire Service," published by the NFPA.

Shaftways

Vertical shafts within buildings sometimes have exterior openings accessible to firefighters. Any such doors or windows should be marked "SHAFTWAY" on the exterior with at least 6 inch high lettering (Figure 2.26) as required by the IFC and NFPA 1. This warns firefighters that this would be an unsafe entry point. If properly marked, time will not be wasted attempting entry at these points.

Normally, interior openings to shafts are readily discernable. Ordinary elevator doors are not likely to be mistaken for anything else. However, other interior shaft openings that could be mistaken for ordinary doors or windows should also have shaftway marking.

Skylights

Without special precautions, roof-mounted skylights obscured by heavy smoke or snow may collapse under the weight of a firefighter. Skylights should be designed to bear the same weight load as the roof. The same applies to coverings over unused skylights. If this is not practical, mount barriers around skylights to prevent firefighters from inadvertently stepping on them.

Considerations – Hazards to the Fire Service
- Provide prominent exterior signs on all buildings with truss construction.
- Mark all exterior shaftway openings.
- Mark all interior shaftway openings that are not readily discernable.
- Never design traps or pitfalls into buildings.
- Use design precautions to prevent falls through skylights.

(Fig. 2.26) Exterior shaftway marking.

Chapter 3
Sprinkler Systems

GENERAL

Sprinkler systems provide early fire control or extinguishment, helping to mitigate the hazards for occupants and firefighters alike. Building codes, fire codes, and life safety codes specify when to provide sprinkler systems. These may be either locally written codes or adopted model codes such as the IBC, the IFC, NFPA 1, NFPA 101, or NFPA 5000. In addition, various sections of the OSHA standards require the installation of sprinkler systems.

A widely accepted installation standard for commercial system design is NFPA 13, Standard for the Installation of Sprinkler Systems. Other standards include: NFPA 13D, Standard for the Installation of Sprinkler Systems in One- and Two-Family Dwellings and Mobile Homes; and NFPA 13R, Standard for the Installation of Sprinkler Systems in Residential Occupancies up to and Including Four Stories in Height. Designers may also refer to NFPA 13E, Recommended Practice for Fire Department Operations in Properties Protected by Sprinkler and Standpipe Systems, although any given fire service organization may follow different standard operating procedures.

There is some flexibility in portions of the system that may impact the fire service. This chapter provides guidance to designers so they may exercise this flexibility to benefit fire department operations. Fire department connections for sprinkler systems are covered in Chapter 5. Standpipe systems (which are often integrated with sprinkler systems) are covered in Chapter 4. Sprinkler designers should also see Chapter 6 for additional guidance on fire alarm annunciation, and Chapter 7 for special coordination considerations about smoke control systems.

ZONING

It is important for sprinkler designers and fire alarm designers to work together, especially in unusual buildings. The fire alarm system will often have an annunciator to indicate the location of the alarm to the fire department. Sprinkler piping arrangement will limit options for fire alarm annunciation of water flow signals. Coordination is essential to furnish the fire service with clear information on the fire or its location.

Sprinkler designers often think in terms of ceiling levels, since sprinkler piping and sprinkler heads usually are at ceilings or roof decks. However, alarm signals are reported in terms of their floor level to enable the fire department to respond to the correct floor during an emergency. Consider the situation of a building with two levels adjacent to a single level "high-bay" area. The first floor sprinkler zone should include both the high bay area and the lower level of the two-level section because each of these areas shares the same floor. Meanwhile, the upper level of the two-story section should have its own zone, even if the piping it contains is on the same level as the high bay area.

In buildings with standpipe systems, sprinkler systems are usually combined with them and fed by a single water supply. Sprinkler systems are fed from the bulk feed mains or from vertical standpipe risers. NFPA 13 requires that sprinkler controls remain independent of standpipe systems. Typically, all sprinklers would be located downstream from a control valve that will not shut off any fire hose connections (Figure 3.1). This enables the fire department to shut off the sprinklers during the rare occasions when a sprinkler pipe fails, or the sprinklers are not controlling the fire. In this manner, hose connections remain available for manual fire suppression without losing pressure from the broken pipe, or the excessive number of activated sprinklers.

In some situations, when a building does not include a standpipe system, NFPA 13 allows fire hose connections to be fed from sprinkler systems. In these cases, closing the sprinkler system valve would shut off the fire hose connections.

In some cases, sprinkler systems are fed from two different standpipes or feed mains, in a "dual-feed" arrangement. Although this provides a hydraulic design advantage, NFPA 13 recommends against it to avoid confusion. If a designer chooses this arrangement (and the code official permits it), cross-reference signs should be provided at each valve. Each of these signs would indicate the location of the companion valve that feeds the same system. No single sprinkler system should be fed from three or more points, since the flow from a single sprinkler may not activate any of the flow switches.

(Fig. 3.1) Sprinkler zone control station and zone indicator sign.

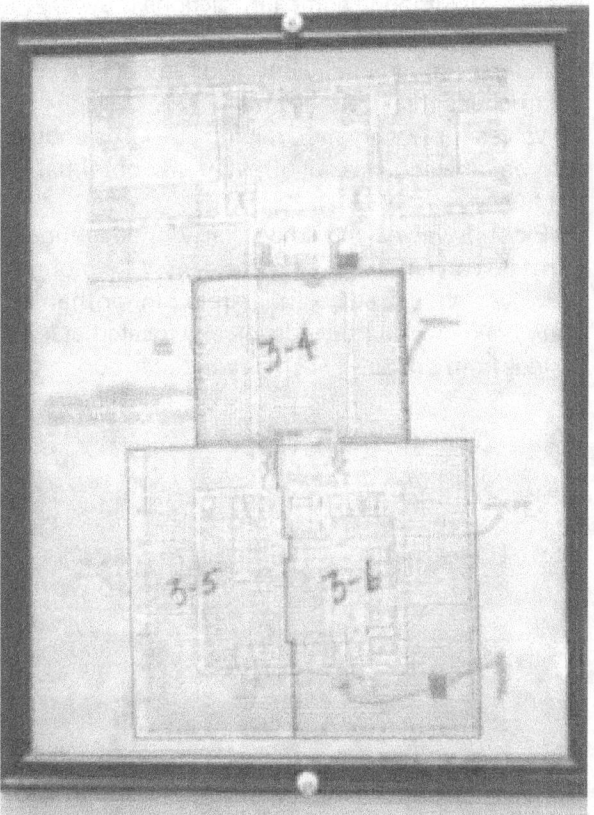

(Fig. 3.2) Sprinkler zone diagram.

Considerations – Sprinkler Zoning
- Coordinate pipe arrangement with fire alarm zoning.
- Keep sprinkler controls independent of standpipe systems.
- Avoid dual feed systems, or provide cross-reference signs.

WATER SUPPLY CONTROL VALVES

Fire service personnel often need rapid access to valves. If a valve is closed during an incident, it may need to be opened to permit flow of water. If a sprinkler valve is open, it may need to be closed to assist in manual suppression efforts.

NFPA 13 requires marking for all water supply control valves including main valves, pump valves, sectional valves, and zone valves. The wording "control valve" by itself does not tell a user the specific use of the valve or what portion of the system is downstream of a particular valve. Using more descriptive labels such as "12th floor" or "pump bypass" will avoid confusion (Figure 3.1).

If a valve identification is not obvious, an additional diagram should be provided. For instance, if a floor has multiple zones, each control valve sign should identify the corresponding zone, such as "12th floor east" or "zone 7-2." A diagram of zones and the boundaries between them should be mounted adjacent to each valve (Figure 3.2). This will enable firefighters to quickly determine which valve controls each specific area.

NFPA 13 requires valves to be accessible for operation. If valves are located in stairs, they will be protected and easily accessible during a fire event.

When a water supply control valve must be located in a room or in a concealed space, a sign outside the door or access panel helps firefighters to quickly locate it (Figure 2.20). If the concealed space is above a suspended ceiling, the appropriate place for the sign is on the fixed ceiling grid, rather than on a removable ceiling tile. In addition, some jurisdictions require exterior signs that indicate the locations of interior valves (Figure 3.3).

Valve handles are often located high enough to be out of vandals' easy reach. However, such placement requires a ladder to reach them when necessary. Although some jurisdictions may require that valves be low enough to reach without a ladder, all minimum height requirements for obstructions must be followed.

Valves for testing and draining purposes should also be labeled. This will prevent any potential confusion.

Exterior valves should be placed in locations accessible even during a fire incident. Wall-mounted valves should be positioned no higher than 5 feet above grade (ground level) and located at least 40 feet from openings such as windows, doors, or vents (Figure 3.4). Post indicator valves should be at least 40 feet from the buildings they serve. The 40 foot distance is called for in NFPA 24.

Designers should require proper notification when their designs require systems, or portions of systems, to be temporarily shut off. This would typically occur during system alterations, or phased installations. In these instances, the design documents should require notification of any system impairments to the responsible fire service organization and coordination with the fire service about any requirements that these impairments may entail.

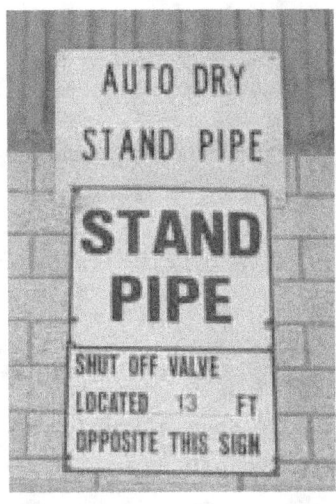

(Fig. 3.3) Exterior sign showing valve location (in this case for a standpipe system).

(Fig. 3.4) Wall control valve next to window. Fire issuing from this window could prevent access to the valve.

Considerations – Water Supply Control Valves
- Label all valves for specific use or area covered.
- Provide diagrams to show boundaries between zones.
- Locate interior valves in enclosed stairs wherever possible.
- Provide signage for valves that are outside stairs or in concealed spaces.
- Provide exterior signs showing the location of interior valves.
- Locate exterior post indicator valves 40 feet from the building.
- Locate exterior wall-mounted valves 40 feet from openings and within 5 feet of grade.

Occupational Safety and Health Administration

FIRE PUMPS

Fire pumps are used to boost the water pressure in sprinkler and standpipe systems and to deliver the required amount of water (Figure 3.5). This is necessary when the system is fed by a non-pressurized water tank, or when the water supply feeding the system has inadequate pressure. A fire pump may be driven by an electric motor, diesel engine, or steam turbine.

(Fig. 3.5) Fire pump.

NFPA 20, Standard for the Installation of Stationary Pumps for Fire Protection, contains design and installation details for fire pump installations. NFPA 20 requires electrical monitoring of pump controllers for pump running, power failure, or controller trouble. These remote alarm signals are often incorporated into fire alarm annunciators, so that fire departments may identify the status of a given fire pump.

A fire pump controller is the enclosure that contains controls and status indicators for a fire pump. NFPA 20 requires these devices to be within sight of the fire pump motor or engine. The automatic transfer switch, which is often in a separate enclosure, transfers power to a secondary power source (when provided). Fire service personnel may need access to this equipment during the course of a fire.

NFPA 20 contains reliability requirements for the power supply to an electrically driven fire pump. For example, power supply lines must be protected and the circuit must be independent of a building's electric service. The latter feature allows the fire service to shut down building power while the fire pump continues to run. 29 CFR Subpart S must also be followed.

The most desirable location for a fire pump is in a separate building. This affords the most protection from fire, and gives firefighters easy access to the pump and its controllers. If locating the pump in a separate building is not possible, a fire-rated room with an outside entrance is the next best option. NFPA 20 requires pump rooms to be separated from the rest of the building by 2-hour fire-rated construction in buildings without full sprinkler protection, and 1-hour construction in fully sprinklered buildings.

Inside and outside entrances to fire pump rooms should be labeled with signage. Minimum lettering size should be six inches high with a 1/2 inch stroke (thickness of lines in each letter).

Considerations – Fire Pumps
- Remote alarms for pumps should be at the fire alarm annunciator, if provided.
- Locate pumps in separate buildings if possible.
- If pumps are in the same building, locate in fire-rated room, preferably with an exterior entrance.
- Mark the entrances to pump rooms.
- Observe special electric power supply requirements.

PARTIAL SPRINKLER SYSTEMS

NFPA 13 requires installation of sprinklers throughout the building. However, in some situations the code or standard requiring sprinklers calls for protecting only a portion of the building. In these cases, exterior signage should indicate the portion of the building covered. A good location for this sign would be at the fire department connection (see the section Marking, page 47).

Residential sprinkler systems installed under NFPA 13D and 13R primarily protect lives rather than property. Since property protection is secondary, large and significant areas may not have sprinkler protection (unsprinklered). One- and two-family houses protected by NFPA 13D systems are readily recognized as having this partial, life-safety type of protection.

Apartments and condominiums with NFPA 13R systems may not be easy to identify. These systems are allowed in buildings four stories or less in height. However, some buildings that are considered four stories in height by building codes may still contain additional levels such as lofts, and basements which may be partially below grade. Several sides of these buildings may have six occupied levels above grade and still be considered four stories in height (Figure 3.6). The large unsprinklered areas can adversely impact firefighter safety and consequently the tactics employed. Fire department ground ladders may not reach the top occupied stories, and some apartment units may not be reached by the available access for aerial ladders. Exterior signage near the fire department connection can alert the fire department to this.

(Fig. 3.6)   This building has six occupied levels from this view. However, it is classified as a four-story building by the code that was in effect during its construction. As such, an NFPA 13R residential sprinkler system (with no sprinklers in the combustible attic or in the floor/ceiling assemblies) protects it.

Considerations – Partial Sprinkler Systems
- NFPA 13 systems: Provide sign near fire department connection showing portion protected.
- NFPA 13R systems: Provide sign near fire department connection indicating the system only covers life hazard areas.

Chapter 4
Standpipe Systems

GENERAL

Standpipe systems consist of a fixed piping system and hose valve connections to preclude the need for long hose lays within tall or large buildings. Water is fed into these systems either through an automatic water supply or manually through a fire department connection. The system delivers water to hose connections throughout the building, usually in enclosed or exterior stairs (Figure 4.1). Firefighters then extend hose lines from these hose connections to conduct interior fire suppression operations. Standpipes are, in effect, a critical component in the supply of water to interior firefighting crews. Deficiencies can have disastrous consequences, such the loss of three firefighters in the 1991 Meridian Plaza fire in Philadelphia.

Systems are classified according to usage: fire department use (Class I), occupant use (Class II), or combined fire department and occupant use (Class III). The use of Class II and III systems has declined over the years due to the training and equipment requirements associated with them. The majority of systems installed today are Class I. Consequently, this chapter will focus on Class I systems.

Building and fire codes specify when designers should incorporate standpipe systems. This can be a locally written code or an adopted model code such as the IBC, the IFC, NFPA 5000, or NFPA 101. Standpipe systems requirements are based on building height or interior travel distances. In addition, standards such as those issued by OSHA require standpipe systems in certain situations.

The IBC and IFC include water supply requirements and some design details. The complete installation standard for standpipe systems is NFPA 14, Standard for the Installation of Standpipe and Hose Systems. This standard allows options for hose connections, valving, and other design features. This chapter illustrates ways that designers can impliment various options in different situations to assist the fire service.

The considerations in the section, Water Supply Control Valves, on page 29, regarding valves also apply to standpipe systems. Fire department connections are covered in Chapter 5 on page 41.

(Fig. 4.1) A dry standpipe in an exterior stair. The FDC inlet is to the right of the building entrance, the riser pipe extends through the left side stair landings, and hose connections are at each level, including the roof.

(Fig. 4.2) Hose connection on intermediate landing as viewed from the main landing where the stair entry door is located.

(Fig. 4.3) Training session showing a firefighter chocking open a stair door to initiate a fire attack from a stairway hose connection.

FIRE HOSE CONNECTIONS

Hose connections in Class I systems are typically 2½ inch threaded outlets. As discussed in the Fire Hydrant section, it is essential that hose connection type and size match that used by the fire department in the jurisdiction where the building is located.

The primary location for hose connections is within enclosed, fire-resistance rated stairs. Firefighters set up and begin their attack from within the protected stair enclosure. Then the attack may proceed towards the fire location. If a quick evacuation becomes necessary, the hose then functions as a lifeline, leading the firefighters back to the protection of the stairs.

The current preferred location for stairway hose connections is at the intermediate stair landings between floors (Figure 4.2). This is because firefighters usually stretch hose from below the fire floor for their protection. If the connections are at intermediate landings, the hose line reaches farther than it would if the connection were at the main landing, a full story below the fire floor. However, both NFPA 14 and the IBC permit connections to be located at main floor landings, if so desired by a given jurisdiction.

If hose valves are located on main landings, consider the position of hose connections in relation to the door. The connections should not be behind the door when it is open. Designers should position the outlet to permit the hose line to run out the door without kinking and without obstructing travel on the stair.

Fire attack using hose lines from stairway hose connections requires stair doors to be propped open (Figure 4.3). This prevents the hose from becoming kinked and restricting water flow; however, it can also allow smoke and heat to enter the stairway. At this point, occupants should either have exited the building, be below the level of the fire, use another stairway, or be sheltered in place until after the incident. But, there is now some concern within the fire protection community that occupants may be exposed to fire or smoke conditions during these firefighting operations. Some reasons for this include: conflicting evacuation instructions, occupants not following evacuation instructions, the need for the fire department to operate from all stairways, or the need for total building evacuation (especially in response to terrorist incidents).

OSHA
Occupational Safety and
Health Administration

One resolution to the dilemma of charged hose lines keeping stair doors open is to place hose connections just outside the stair door instead of inside the stair enclosure (Figure 4.4). However, this is not recommended because such a design forces the fire attack to begin without the protection of the stair enclosure and eliminates the lifeline concept. A better solution is to place additional hose valves just outside the stair door to give firefighters the option of connecting hose lines to these or to the connections within the stair enclosure. The connection outside the stair can be 1½ inches in size to facilitate initial fire attack with smaller size hose lines during occupant evacuation. This should suffice for most fire situations in buildings with a complete operable sprinkler system. However, some fire departments do not use small sized hose lines for standpipe operations. In those cases, any additional hose connections would also need to be 2½ inches in size.

Another approach to maintaining the integrity of stair enclosures during fire suppression operations is to place hose connections in a fire-rated vestibule between the stairs and the building interior. Although such vestibules require a little more room, they can double as refuge areas for individuals with mobility impairments. If the vestibules are open to the exterior, any smoke that does migrate into them will dissipate easily (Figure 4.5).

If the location of stairs precludes hose lines from reaching the farthest points of a particular floor, the designer should include remote (or supplemental) hose connections. NFPA 14 limits travel distance to 150 feet in buildings that do not have complete sprinkler protection, and to 200 feet in fully sprinklered buildings. In buildings with a corridor system feeding multiple rooms, tenants, or agencies, designers should locate remote hose stations within the corridor. Often a corridor's walls, ceilings, doors, and other openings will be rated for fire or smoke resistance. If so, they provide some degree of protection for firefighters, although it is usually less than that provided by a stairway enclosure. In any case, the least desirable place for remote hose connections is within suites or tenant spaces.

(Fig. 4.4) Hose connection on the corridor side of the stair door.

(Fig. 4.5) Exterior view of open air vestibules between the stair and the interior of a building.

Remote hose connections outside of stairwells can often be hard to locate. They should be placed as uniformly as possible on all floors to make them easier to find. Highly visible signs or other markings can assist firefighters in locating them quickly (Figures 4.6 and 4.9). Often these may be tailored to décor or occupancy to satisfy architects or interior designers (Figures 4.7 and 4.8). NFPA 170, Standard for Symbols for Use by the Fire Service, contains symbols for marking standpipe outlets (hose connections).

Placement of remote hose connections can also affect their accessibility. For instance, in parking garages designers should try to locate hose connections adjacent to drive aisles. Where they are intermingled with parking spaces, an access path at least three feet wide delineated with bollards or a raised, curbed area should be provided to preclude cars from obstructing the connection (Figure 4.9).

(Fig. 4.6) Stripe on column to identify hose connection location in a parking garage.

Considerations - Fire Hose Connections
- Determine if connections are to be on intermediate or main stair landings.
- Investigate feasibility of additional connections just outside stair doors or locating connections in vestibules.
- Locate supplemental hose connections uniformly in corridors.
- Use curbed raised access path to connections in parking garages.
- Mark supplemental connections clearly.
- Make sure hose threads are compatible.

(Fig. 4.7) Sign to identify hose connection location in an exhibit hall.

OSHA
Occupational Safety and
Health Administration

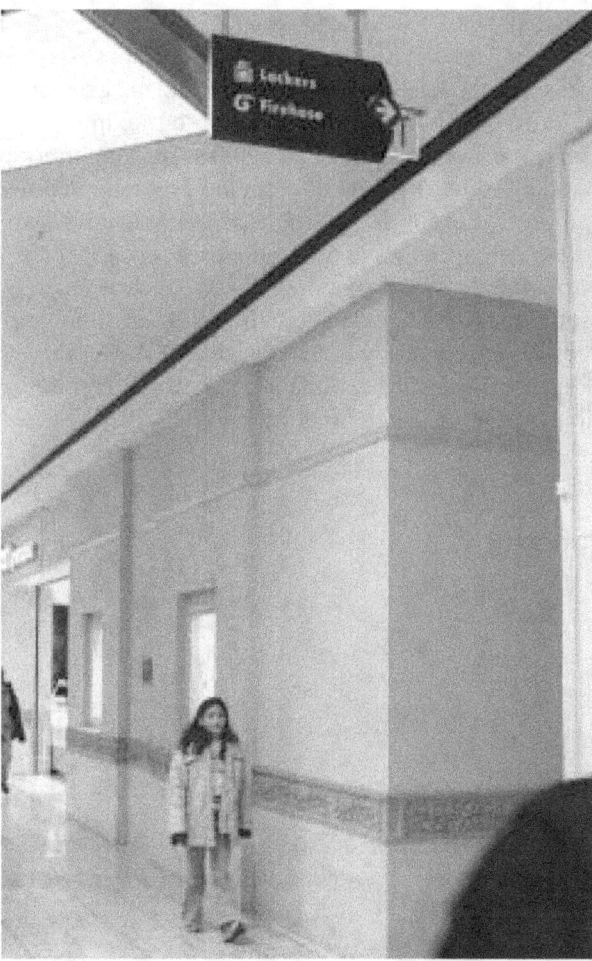

(Fig. 4.8) Sign to identify hose connection location in a shopping mall.

(Fig. 4.9) Bollards and striping to create an access path in a parking garage. Bright signs at the top of column help to locate the valve.

DESIGN PRESSURE

Most new standpipe systems are designed by hydraulic calculations. This ensures that the water supply, pipe sizes used, and pumps (if needed) will provide a certain flow and pressure at a specified number of hose connections in the system. The current NFPA 14 specifies a minimum design pressure for Class I systems of 100 pounds per square inch (psi) at a specific flow rate, which depends on the number of hose connections per floor. However, it includes an exception that allows design pressures as low as 65 psi, if this will accommodate the fire suppression tactics.

These minimum pressures are based on certain assumptions about the fire department equipment and tactics, as well as the fixed fire pump feeding the standpipe system. The designer should compensate if the equipment or tactics vary from these assumptions in a particular building or jurisdiction. This will ensure the adequacy of fire streams to assure the safety of firefighters conducting interior operations.

A straight stream nozzle requires at least 50 psi to operate. With the friction loss in fire hose added, 65 psi at the hose connection will provide 50 psi to a straight stream nozzle with 250 gallons per minute (gpm) flowing through 100 feet of 2½ inch fire hose. The same pressures can deliver 95 gpm through 100 feet of 1¾ inch hose.

In 1993, NFPA 14 changed the minimum required design pressure from 65 psi to 100 psi at the hose connections. At the same time, this standard was revised to permit longer distances between hose connections and remote areas of a building. Currently, this distance can be up to 150 feet for buildings without complete sprinkler protection, and up to 200 feet for fully sprinklered buildings. The 100 psi design pressure will permit greater flows or longer hose lines, but only with the same straight stream nozzles.

Many fire service organizations begin their attacks with fog or combination nozzles that generally require at least 100 psi to operate. This dramatically increases the pressure requirements at the hose connection. If 100 psi is actually available at the connection, every combination of hose size and length will result in inadequate nozzle pressure. It is assumed that firefighters will use fog or combination nozzles early in a fire situation, when only one or two hose lines are in operation. It is further assumed that the total flow will be less than the rated flow of the pump. At these lower flows, output pressures will be higher. Finally, it is assumed that if the fire grows, either straight stream nozzles will be utilized or the pumpers supplying the fire department connections will provide greater pressures.

Designers must be aware of this information for a number of reasons. First, designers should only use 65 psi minimum design pressure when a particular fire department so specifies, based on their equipment and tactics. An example would be if a department used only 2½ inch hose and straight stream nozzles for standpipe operations. Other design conditions such as additional fire hose connections to enable shorter hose lines may also factor into the decision.

In all cases where lower pressure is not specifically approved by the fire department, 100 psi basic pressure should be considered the minimum. However, if any of the above assumptions about the fire pump or the fire department equipment and tactics are invalid in a particular building or jurisdiction, designers should consider providing pressures greater than the basic 100 psi at the hose connections to facilitate adequate fire streams.

NFPA 14 imposes a maximum pressure limit of 175 psi on standpipe systems for fire department use. Pressures in excess of 175 psi will invoke requirements for pressure reducing devices, which are covered in the next section, Pressure Regulating Devices.

Considerations – Design Pressure
- Use minimum 100 psi outlet pressure unless specifically exempted by the fire department, with justification based on tactics.
- If fog or combination nozzles are used for standpipe operations, investigate fire department procedures and tactics to check the need for pressures over 100 psi (but not exceeding 175 psi).

PRESSURE REGULATING DEVICES

Pressure regulating devices (PRDs) restrict system pressures, usually below 175 psi for Class I systems (Figure 4.10). This is considered the maximum safe operating pressure as well as the maximum working pressure limit of most fire protection components. Proper design of PRDs is imperative so that firefighters have adequate pressure for hose streams. As a stark example, failure to coordinate settings on these devices with fire department tactics emerged as a key issue in the 1991 Meridian Plaza high-rise fire in Philadelphia, which resulted in the death of three firefighters.

(Fig. 4.10) Hose connection equipped with a pressure regulating device.

PRDs fall into three categories: pressure reducing valves (PRVs), pressure control valves, and pressure restricting devices. Pressure restricting devices do not limit pressure during static (non-flowing) conditions, nor do they maintain a constant discharge pressure. These devices incorporate orifice plates, mechanical pressure restrictors, or valve limiting stops. Pressure restricting devices are not used for new Class I standpipe systems. However, designers may encounter these when redesigning existing systems, which would provide the opportunity to implement some or all of the considerations below.

PRVs and pressure control valves limit both static and residual (flowing) pressures. However, many of these valves are factory preset to attain specific outlet pressures with specific inlet pressures. It is important for designers to specify the inlet pressure range for valves as well as the desired outlet pressure, so that they may be designed properly and then installed on the correct floors. Careful attention during design, installation, acceptance testing, and maintenance ensures that systems with PRDs will function properly.

Occupational Safety and Health Administration

PRVs and pressure control valves have other disadvantages. Their failure rate has been high, resulting in the addition of testing requirements to NFPA 14. Secondly, many cannot be adjusted by firefighters during a fire, or they require special tools and knowledge. Finally, hose connections with these devices cannot be used as backup fire department inlet connections, since water can only flow through a PRD in one direction.

The most reliable means of limiting pressures in standpipe systems is to design them to preclude the need for pressure regulating devices. In shorter buildings, careful attention to the design of pumps and the maximum pressure supplied by incoming water mains can accomplish this. In taller buildings, the same concept can be applied to each separate vertical standpipe zone. Pressure fluctuations in the water supply as well as the full range of fire pump capacity are essential considerations in any building.

If the use of PRDs cannot be avoided, certain design features will balance their disadvantages. The easier the valves are to adjust in the field, the faster the fire service can overcome any unforeseen situation. Designers should select valves which can be easily adjusted and specify that identification signs and adjustment instructions be posted at each valve. The tools required to perform field adjustments should be kept in a secure yet accessible location such as the fire command center or a locked cabinet near the fire alarm annunciator. Finally, a supplemental system inlet should be provided at the level of fire department entry. This can be simply an extra hose connection without a PRD on a riser. NFPA 14 recommends a supplemental inlet, and it is especially important for systems with a single fire department connection.

Considerations - Pressure Regulating Devices
- Design to preclude the need for PRDs.
- Specify the highest and lowest possible inlet pressures at each PRD location.
- Select devices capable of simple emergency adjustment.
- Post identification signs and adjustment instructions.
- Provide adjustment tools in a secure, accessible location.
- Provide backup inlet connection at fire department entry level.

STANDPIPE ISOLATION VALVES

The considerations in the section, Water Supply Control Valves, on page 29, apply to standpipe systems as well. This section gives additional guidance on valves specific to standpipe systems.

The vertical pipes that feed hose connections are called standpipes or risers. If there are multiple risers, NFPA 14 requires interconnections with supply piping to form a single system, with valves at the point where each riser is fed by the main bulk piping coming from the water supply point. Designers should also put valves on the feed lines to remote or supplemental hose connections (see Fire Hose Connections, page 34).

These valves are all called "standpipe isolation valves." The ones on vertical risers are called "riser isolation valves." They allow the fire department to shut off, or isolate, any given riser or feed that breaks or otherwise fails. Firefighters may then use the remaining standpipes.

(Fig. 4.11) Isolation valve between the feed main (entering from the lower left) and the vertical riser (on the right). It is located within the stair enclosure for protection. The valve at the top of the photo is a sprinkler zone control valve.

NFPA 14 requires that riser isolation valves separately control the feed to each standpipe (Figure 4.11). Sequential valves are not acceptable where a single valve in the bulk main can shut off more than one downstream riser. For risers in stairways, the riser isolation valves should be within the fire-rated stair enclosure to protect firefighters who may need to operate them.

Previous editions of NFPA 14 required designers to place the riser isolation valves at the bottom of the risers to make them quickly accessible to firefighters. Fire departments may still prefer that these valves be located on the level that they use for their primary entry. If the bulk feed main is located on a different level it could be piped up or down to the fire department entry level, where the isolation valve would be placed for that particular riser (Figure 4.12).

Considerations - Standpipe Isolation Valves
- Provide a separate valve on each riser for independent control.
- Locate valves for risers in stairs within the stair enclosure.
- Locate valves on fire department entry level.

(Fig. 4.12)   The feed for this standpipe was on a level above the fire department entry. The supply pipe was fed down (on the left) to the entry level, where the isolation valve was located. Then, the pipe was routed back upwards (on the right) to feed the standpipe riser.

OTHER DESIGN ISSUES

Standpipes should be installed as the construction of a building progresses. These can be temporary or permanent. Both the IFC and NFPA 241, Standard for Safeguarding Construction, Alteration, and Demolition Operations, contain requirements for standpipes during construction. Design documents should indicate the applicable requirements. A marked, accessible fire department connection (see the section, Marking, page 47) can suffice as a water supply until building construction progresses to the point at which the water supply system and fire department pumpers can no longer provide adequate pressure to the system. At this point, a temporary or permanent fire pump also becomes necessary.

In climates subject to freezing temperatures, it is vital that standpipes in unheated areas be dry type systems. Heat tracing and insulation are ineffective protection for dry fire protection systems because water is not normally flowing through the piping.

Large dry systems deserve special considerations. As the size of a dry system increases, the time required to deliver water to the remote hose connection increases. This is due to the increased pipe volume that must be filled. This can be mitigated by subdividing the system into smaller independent systems, or zones. The disadvantage is that fire department inlet connections to dry systems cannot be interconnected (Figure 4.13). See the section, Marking, page 47, for specific recommendations regarding zone indicator signs or diagrams.

Considerations - Other Design Issues
- Specify temporary standpipes during construction.
- Specify installation of the pump when height exceeds fire department capability.
- Design to mitigate long fill times for dry standpipe systems.

(Fig. 4.13) FDCs for separate manual dry standpipe systems in a large parking garage.

Occupational Safety and Health Administration

Chapter 5
Fire Department
Connections

GENERAL

A fire department connection (FDC) includes one or more fire hose inlet connections on a sprinkler system, standpipe system, or other water-based suppression system. The hose inlet connections enable the fire department or fire brigade to hook up hose lines from one or more pumpers and feed water into the system to supplement the connected automatic water supply (Figure 5.1). In manual dry standpipe systems, FDCs are the only water supply.

Requirements for FDCs appear in the following standards:

- NFPA 13, Standard for the Installation of Sprinkler Systems;
- NFPA 13R, Standard for the Installation of Sprinkler Systems in Residential Occupancies up to and Including Four Stories in Height;
- NFPA 14, Standard for the Installation of Standpipe and Hose Systems;
- NFPA 15, Standard for Water Spray Fixed Systems for Fire Protection;
- NFPA 16, Standard for the Installation of Foam-Water Sprinkler and Foam-Water Spray Systems; and
- NFPA 750, Standard on Water Mist Fire Protection Systems.

These standards set minimum criteria for FDCs, such as which systems require them, their arrangement, and the pipe sizes they feed. The IBC and IFC also contain requirements for FDC location and signage. This chapter will expand upon those criteria and provide guidance on FDC location, quantity, numbers of inlets, positioning, and marking. Also included are particular considerations that need to be taken into account during the building construction phase.

In some cases, FDCs are not required because they would be of little or no value. Examples include remote buildings that are inaccessible to the fire service, large open-sprinkler deluge systems that exceed the pumping capability of the fire department, and very small buildings.

Designers should always seek out and follow fire department requirements, recommendations, and advice for special circumstances. The sole users of FDCs are the fire departments that must connect to them. Any deficiency related to the FDC can cause delays in fire suppression, and therefore a decrease in the safety of both firefighters and building occupants.

(Fig. 5.1) Charged hose lines connected to a wall-mounted FDC. The proximity of an FDC relative to building exits is discussed in the Location section at page 44.

QUANTITY

The above standards generally require a single FDC such as the one in Figure 5.1. In some cases, an additional interconnected FDC will be required. For example, NFPA 14 requires multiple FDCs in remote locations on high-rise buildings. This code provision was added after experience with high-rise fires showed that broken glass and debris falling from a fire area can damage hose lines. A second remote FDC increases the dependability of the water supply.

The following section discusses the number of inlets provided for each FDC. However, this decision can be related to the quantity of FDCs. If the water quantity demand of the system is high enough to justify more than two inlets, then the designer should specify separate FDCs. This configuration would facilitate different pumpers feeding different FDCs.

When a building has multiple FDCs, most fire departments would prefer that they be interconnected. This enables the fire department to feed any system from any FDC (Figure 5.2). However, sometimes this is not possible. For example, a manual dry standpipe system (with no connected water supply) cannot be interconnected with an automatic sprinkler system. Sometimes, FDC interconnection is not preferable, as discussed in the section, Other Design Issues, page 40, regarding large dry standpipe systems. When FDCs are not interconnected, the designer should consider special signage as discussed in the section, Marking, on page 47.

(Fig. 5.2) Separate sprinkler and standpipe connections (threaded types). To feed both systems, at least one hose line must be connected to each of the two FDCs.

(Fig. 5.3) A 4-inlet FDC. It would probably be more efficient, and give the fire department more options, to have placed two, 2-inlet FDCs in different locations on this building.

(Fig. 5.4) A quick-connect type of FDC.

Considerations – FDC Quantity
- Provide the required or appropriate number of FDCs.
- When more than two inlets are provided, consider separate FDCs.
- Separate FDCs should be located remotely from one another.
- Interconnect separate FDCs to feed all systems where possible.

Occupational Safety and Health Administration

INLETS

Most standards do not specify the number of inlets required on each FDC. NFPA 13 does say that a single inlet is acceptable for FDCs feeding pipe that is 3 inches or smaller. However, no requirements are identified beyond that. Many FDCs have dual inlets; these are often referred to as "siamese" connections. One rule of thumb is to provide one inlet for each 250 gallons per minute (gpm) of system demand, rounded up to the next highest increment of 250 gpm. For example, if the system demand is 700 gpm, the designer would specify three inlets. Likewise, a system with a demand of 800 gpm would need four inlets (Figure 5.3).

To permit the connection of hoselines, the inlet size and type (threaded or quick-connect) must match the type used by the particular fire department. In jurisdictions where the fire service uses threaded hose couplings, FDCs include one or more 2½ inch-size hose inlets (Figure 5.2). The thread type will usually be NH Type (American National Fire Hose Connection Screw Thread). To facilitate the connection of the externally threaded (male) end of fire hose lines, threaded inlets should be the swiveling, internally threaded (female) type. The non-threaded connections will usually be 4 or 5 inches in size (Figure 5.4).

NFPA 1963, the Standard for Fire Hose Connections, sets out specific detailed requirements for both threaded and non-threaded (quick-connect) hose connections.

The inlets are ordinarily required to be provided with threaded plugs or breakaway-style caps. It is important for the designer to specify these to minimize the chance of an inlet being obstructed by trash or debris. If a firefighter notices an inlet blocked by debris, connection of hose lines will be delayed while he or she attempts to clear it. If the debris cannot be removed, that particular inlet or the entire FDC may be rendered unusable. Unnoticed debris could block most of the flow to a fire hose connection or a significant section of a sprinkler system. Even worse, a firefighter could be operating a hose line inside and suddenly have the blockage clog the nozzle.

Designers may specify lockable inlet caps for security. Designers should obtain permission from the fire department to use these caps, unless the department requires their use. In addition, designers should specify that building owners provide tools or keys for unlocking these caps to the fire department.

Considerations – FDC Inlets
- Match type of connection and thread type to the fire department's hose.
- Provide caps or plugs for each inlet.
- Security caps: Obtain permission if optional and specify that building owners give keys to the fire department.
- Large capacity systems should have one 2½ inch inlet for each 250 gpm of system demand, unless a large capacity, quick-connect FDC is used.

LOCATION

NFPA standards contain performance language regarding the accessibility of FDCs and the ease with which hose lines can be connected. How the designer meets these requirements can streamline fire department operations.

The IBC and IFC specifically require that fire departments approve FDC locations. It is important for designers to seek and obtain this approval.

Both NFPA 13 and 14 require that FDCs be on the "street side" of buildings. The intent is to make them immediately accessible to approaching fire apparatus. The street side is obvious in urban settings where buildings front directly onto the streets. However, for buildings set back from the street, the street side may be subject to interpretation. In these cases, the designer should consult fire department officials about apparatus approach direction and operational procedures.

Another consideration is the location of FDCs in relation to nearby fire hydrants or other water supply sources, (such as tanks, ponds, or lakes). Some jurisdictions require FDCs to be within a certain dis-

(Fig. 5.6) This FDC is mounted too close to a wall. Other obstructions could be fences, pipes, downspouts, vegetation, etc.

tance of the closest fire hydrant. This allows a pumper to hook up directly to a hydrant with its suction hose and then use a pre-connected hose line to quickly feed the FDC (Figure 5.5). For example, if pumpers in a jurisdiction each carry a 150-foot pre-connected 2½ inch hose line, a maximum distance of 100 feet will enable firefighters to manually stretch this hose to the FDC, regardless of the position of the pumper at the hydrant. If there are multiple FDCs, each should meet this distance requirement from separate hydrants to allow for completely redundant operations.

An adequate amount of working room surrounding the FDC will enable a firefighter to approach and connect hose lines. If the inlets are straight-type (perpendicular to the wall), a clear path approximately four feet wide would accommodate the firefighter and the hose lines. If the inlets are angled-type, a clear distance of approximately three feet on each side of the FDC will prevent hose lines from kinking (and restricting flow) when they are charged (Figure 5.6).

The designer should consider site conditions leading to the FDC to make it easier for firefighters to stretch hose lines to it. Sidewalks, steps, grassy areas, or low ground cover will not slow down this process. However, if a firefighter needs to negotiate walls, climb a ladder, maneuver

(Fig. 5.5) FDC on street side of building. A firefighter is stretching a hose line to an FDC after the pumper has been spotted at a nearby hydrant. Also, close at hand are the main entrance and the key box which the officer is unlocking.

around a fence or hedgerow, or cut away a bush, the operation will be delayed. Designers should consider the potential growth of nearby bushes or plants.

Locations that are likely to be blocked should be avoided. Loading docks, by their nature, are subject to temporary storage and vehicular traffic. Another example of a poor location would be in front of a supermarket or department store where stock or carts may block the FDC at any time (Figure 5.7). This may be a good reason to deviate from the "street front" requirement, or to locate the FDC in a column abutting the road (Figure 2.2). Designers should always keep in mind how the building will be used, not just how a particular item will look on the construction plans (devoid of people and equipment).

Designers should pay special attention to hazardous materials. They should locate FDCs away from fuel tanks, gas meters, or other highly flammable or explosive substances or processes (Figures 5.7 and 5.8).

The designer should also consider the locations of entrances and exits when locating FDCs. A charged hose line is very rigid and will block an outward-swinging door, or provide a trip hazard for exiting occupants and entering firefighters (Figure 5.1). Avoid locating FDCs with their inlets pointed in

(Fig. 5.8) This FDC is located too close to the gas service and meter. The breakaway caps make it necessary for a firefighter to swing an axe or other tool to remove these caps. This is an accident waiting to happen that could be avoided through careful design coordination.

(Fig. 5.7) FDC in the cart area of a supermarket entryway. The FDC is located where merchandise or shopping carts could easily block it, or a fire in the adjacent propane storage area could restrict its use.

(Fig. 5.9) An FDC pointed directly across the main entrance of a restaurant. A connected and charged hose line would impede both egress and entry.

the direction of doors, so that firefighter access and occupant egress is not impeded (Figure 5.9).

A freestanding FDC (such as the one shown in Figure 5.11), is an option as long as it is acceptable to the local fire department. Designers may position these anywhere on the property. If an FDC is located far from the building it feeds, consider the special signage discussed in the section, Marking, page 47.

FDCs subject to vehicle damage should be protected by barricades such as the bollards often used near fire hydrants (Figure 2.14). An alternative to protect wall-mounted FDCs is a wall-mounted guard (Figure 5.3).

Considerations – FDC Location
- Locate on street side of buildings, or on line of approach, if building is set back.
- Locate within an easy hose line stretch of a hydrant.
- Locate where it may be easily reached by a firefighter with a hose line.
- Provide at least a 4-foot clear path to the FDC.
- FDCs with angled inlets should have 3 feet of clearance on either side.
- Avoid locations where the FDC may be blocked by area use, e.g., merchandise, storage, equipment, vehicles, etc.
- Avoid areas adjacent to hazardous materials.

POSITION

The Appendix of NFPA 13 recommends that FDCs be installed so that the centerlines of the inlets are between 18 and 48 inches above the adjacent ground. This height will make hose line connection straightforward. Some jurisdictions may prefer a maximum height of 42 inches, or even 36 inches.

Designers should position FDCs based on the final grade, rather than the reverse. If the grade is built up in one area with a mound of soil or mulch to achieve the correct height, this can easily be inadvertently changed later by a landscaper. Or, if a platform is built to achieve the correct height, a fall hazard is created for firefighters who may be working in the dark and/or in smoky conditions (Figure 5.10).

Wall-mounted FDCs should be positioned at least 40 feet away from windows, doors, or vents. This will minimize the chance that fire, heat, or smoke will make it difficult to connect hose lines.

Considerations – FDC Position
- Meet all requirements or recommendations for height above grade.
- Do not use platforms or other artificial means to achieve the correct height.
- Position at least 40 feet from openings when possible.

(Fig. 5.10) A platform built up to reach an FDC creates a hazardous condition. This should not be considered as equivalent to positioning the FDC at a proper height above grade level.

MARKING

NFPA 13 and NFPA 14 require that a small sign with one-inch raised letters be provided on each FDC to identify the type of system (such as sprinkler, standpipe, or combined). These are frequently cast into the plate surrounding the inlets with raised lettering.

Some jurisdictions require or prefer more prominent marking. Larger signs can be visible to firefighters and pumper drivers from farther away. Icons may be provided to indicate whether the connection feeds sprinklers, standpipes, or both. One example of standard signage for this type of use can be found in NFPA 170, Standard for Fire Safety Symbols (Figure 5.11). Prominent signs can help greatly where the FDC is on a building set back from the street. Some jurisdictions require a light to help identify the FDC's location in the dark.

Pump operators are normally trained to supply a certain amount of water pressure to the FDC to augment the system. For example, standard procedure could be to pump sprinkler systems at 125 pounds per square inch (psi), and standpipe systems at 150 psi. Firefighters may adjust this to provide additional pressure to a higher elevation in a given building, or to account for different hose line configurations on standpipe systems. When a sprinkler system requires 150 psi or more to function properly, NFPA 13 requires that a sign indicate the required pressure. Such a sign alerts the pump operator to this unusual condition.

A designer should consider specifying additional FDC signage for underground buildings or transit system facilities. This is because the visual cues that a pump operator typically has on aboveground buildings (such as size or height), are absent. Also, smoke or fire venting provides no indication about the subsurface level where the fire is located. In these cases, a sign indicating the maximum depth and longest horizontal run of pipe gives a pump operator an idea of the pressure he or she must provide to reach the most remote areas of the system (Figure 5.12).

(Fig. 5.12) A nameplate on an underground transit system facility, showing the depth and maximum horizontal run of standpipe feed piping.

(Fig. 5.11) FDC sign with an NFPA 170 symbol for both sprinkler and standpipe systems.

(Fig. 5.13) Address indicator sign to show which building this FDC feeds.

In some circumstances, an FDC will feed a system covering only a portion of the building. Signage at the FDC indicating such partial protection alerts responding firefighters to this, so they may factor it into their risk analysis. Signage should provide enough detail so that firefighters connecting the hose lines can identify the proper connection.

There are also situations (discussed in the sections, Other Design Issues, page 40 and, Quantity, page 42) where multiple FDCs on a building are not interconnected. In these cases, designers should consider the signage to assist the fire department in supplying the correct FDC. Diagrammatic signs are visually the most helpful.

FDCs that are far from the buildings they feed also need special signs. If multiple buildings and the FDC locations make it unclear which FDC goes to which building, designers should provide appropriate identification (Figure 5.13).

Considerations – FDC Marking
- Mark FDCs prominently when remote from fire apparatus access.
- Add signage for systems with a demand pressure over 150 psi.
- Add signage for underground buildings and facilities.
- Mark partial systems (preferably with a diagrammatic sign).
- Mark sections of non-interconnected systems (preferably with a diagrammatic sign).
- Add signage if the corresponding building is not clearly obvious.

OSHA
Occupational Safety and
Health Administration

TEMPORARY CONNECTIONS

Designers should consider the location and marking of temporary FDCs for temporary standpipes to assist the fire service. The section, Other Design Issues, on page 40, discusses temporary standpipes during construction or demolition.

When specifying the location of a temporary FDC, the designer should consider using areas around the construction site perimeter. If the FDC is located well away from areas likely to be used for storage, unloading, and heavy equipment such as cranes, it is more likely to be accessible to the fire service (Figure 5.14).

The designer should also coordinate the temporary FDC location with any planned construction barricades. Fire service operations will be delayed if walls or fences need to be breached to supply the FDC.

Very prominent signs should mark the locations of temporary FDCs. During construction, aesthetics are not of great importance. A large, brightly colored sign with "FDC" painted in a contrasting color will help the fire service locate the FDC rapidly amid the clutter of a construction site (Figure 5.15). Designers should also specify the removal of the sign when the temporary FDC is removed.

(Fig. 5.15) A temporary FDC labeled with a large colorful sign, as well as large letters "FDC" spray-painted on the building.

Considerations – Temporary FDCs
- Coordinate FDC locations with areas likely to be blocked during construction.
- Mark FDC location with very large, brightly colored signs.

(Fig. 5.14) This is a building under construction as viewed from a piece of fire apparatus turning the corner onto the block. Can you see the FDC? It is not labeled, and it is blocked by a vehicle, a trash container, a fence, and construction materials. It is directly above the car's front bumper.

Chapter 6
Fire Alarm and
Communication Systems

GENERAL

A fire alarm system consists of interconnected devices and controls to alert building occupants to fire or dangerous conditions and provide emergency responders with information on those conditions. Clear and concise information will enable responders to operate efficiently and safely.

Fire alarm systems monitor alarm-initiating devices such as manual pull stations, automatic detectors, or water flow indicators (Figure 6.1a). If a signal is received, the control components process it via software programs or relays (Figure 6.1b). The system then activates audible and visual evacuation notification devices (Figure 6.1c); sends a remote signal to the fire service or other authorities; displays the location of the alarm; recalls elevators; and controls ventilation systems.

Systems can vary widely in complexity. A basic, fundamental system consists of a control panel, initiating devices, and notification devices. On the other end of the spectrum are complex selective voice evacuation systems with integrated fire department phone communications systems. Detection systems have devices that automatically sense fire or its byproducts. Detection systems are often integrated into fire alarm systems, and this chapter covers both.

Building and fire codes often specify requirements for fire alarms systems. Commonly used codes include the IBC, NFPA 5000, and NFPA 101. The National Fire Alarm Code, NFPA 72, is a comprehensive installation standard. This code, along with the fire alarm wiring portion of the National Electric Code, NFPA 70, sets the requirements for design, installation, and maintenance. In addition, OSHA standards create obligations with respect to employee alarm systems.

This chapter covers fire service personnel interaction with fire alarm systems and provides guidance for designers to facilitate operational efficiency. Elevator control, often interconnected with the fire alarm system, is discussed in the section, Firefighter Access, on page 21. The section, Smoke Control Systems, on page 63, covers these systems.

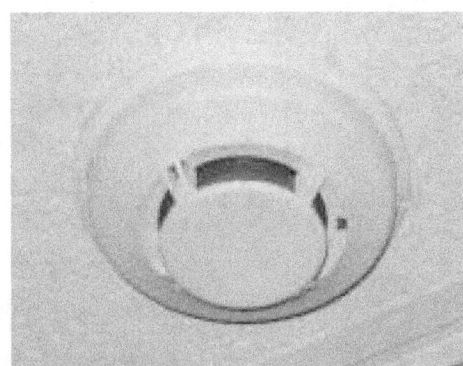

(Fig. 6.1a) Initiating device (smoke detector).

(Fig. 6.1b) Control panel.

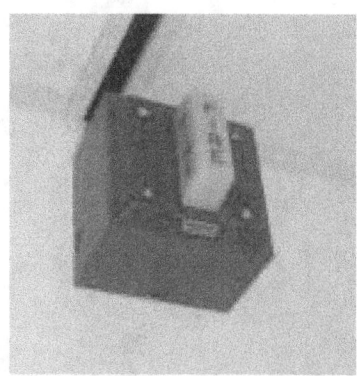

(Fig. 6.1c) Notification device (horn/strobe).

ZONING AND ANNUNCIATION

An annunciator panel displays information about the location and type of alarm. This assists the fire service with their initial response and may help track the spread of smoke or heat. A building may have multiple annunciators to serve multiple entrances. Or, there may be different annunciators for different users, such as the fire department, the security force, and building management staff. This manual focuses on annunciator features applicable to fire service use. Designers should always consult the fire department on the design and location of these devices.

The location of an annunciator is critical to its usefulness. Typically, the best location is at the main entrance where the fire department plans to initially respond. In some large buildings, it may be beneficial to have duplicate annunciators at different locations. For buildings, such as high-rises with fire control rooms, the annunciator is usually located within these rooms. However, depending on the room's accessibility, designers may choose to place an additional annunciator at the main entrance.

Each building should have its own annunciator, even if a single fire alarm control system serves multiple buildings. Fire service operations would be delayed if it were necessary for one unit to report to a given building to check the annunciator, then relocate (or direct another unit) to investigate origination of the alarm. In large complexes, an additional master annunciator could assist the fire service in locating the building where an alarm originates.

Annunciators display alarm information in different ways. Some have lights or LEDs that are labeled (Figure 6.2). Alphanumeric annunciators have a readout-type display that may be programmed to show very specific information describing the alarm signal (Figure 6.3). A printer is yet another means of annunciation. It is usually used in conjunction with other devices. In very simple systems, the control panel serves as the annunciator. In such cases, its location and features should meet all annunciator requirements.

(Fig. 6.3) Control panel with alphanumeric annunciation display.

(Fig. 6.2) Simple fire alarm control panel with lamps and zone labels for annunciation.

The annunciator panel may also store building plans and diagrams. These are then quickly accessible to firefighters. A note outside the panel can indicate that it contains building plans or diagrams.

All annunciators include:
- Floor: the level where the signal originated;
- Zone: the area where the signal originated; and
- Device: the type of alarm or supervisory initiating device.

Local fire or building codes may dictate zone size. The annex of NFPA 72 specifies a maximum zone size of 20,000 square feet and 300 linear feet. The zone limitations in both the IBC and NFPA 5000 are 22,500 square feet and 300 linear feet. Zone boundaries should coincide with fire ratings, smoke ratings, or building-use boundaries.

Zone descriptors, whether labels next to lamps or alphanumeric displays, should provide pertinent information to fire service personnel. Designers should assume that users will not be familiar with the building. Descriptors should be intuitive and rapidly decipherable. As the building, layout, tenants, or room names change, building owners should update descriptions.

Flow switches or pressure switches indicate water flow. To direct the fire department to the appropriate area, it is important that the zone indication show the area covered by the sprinkler system. The location of the switch itself is not important for fire department response operations.

Alarm devices indicate a situation requiring emergency action and normally activate evacuation signals.

Examples of Alarm Devices:
- Manual pull station
- Sprinkler flow
- Smoke detector
- Heat detector
- Kitchen cooking equipment extinguishing system
- Clean agent system
- Carbon dioxide system
- Halon system

Smoke and heat detectors should be further identified on the annunciator by mounting location:
- Area (ceiling)
- Underfloor
- Duct
- Air plenum
- Elevator lobby
- Elevator machine room
- Elevator hoistway
- Stair shaft

Supervisory devices indicate abnormal conditions. They signal a need for non-emergency action, such as repair, and they should not cause an evacuation alarm or notify the fire department.

Examples of Supervisory Devices:
- Valve tamper switch (closed or partially closed water supply control valve)
- Dry sprinkler high or low air pressure switch
- Pre-action sprinkler low air pressure switch
- Water tank low temperature or low water level indicator
- Valve room low air temperature indicator

Some devices control certain building features, such as fans, doors, or dampers. They may be shown as "alarm" or "supervisory," depending on the preference of the code official.

Examples of Alarm or Supervisory Devices:
- Duct smoke detectors
- Air plenum smoke detectors
- Underfloor detectors
- Door closure smoke detectors
- Elevator hoistway smoke detectors
- Elevator machine room smoke detectors
- Heat detectors for elevator shutdown
- Stair smoke detectors

Note: Some jurisdictions require devices that are subject to unwanted alarms (primarily duct or air plenum smoke detectors) be supervisory.

Status indicators give information about whether the main fire alarm power is on, or they report on the condition of devices external to the alarm system.

Examples of Status Indicators:
- Main system power on
- Main system trouble
- Fire pump running
- Fire pump fault,
- Fire pump phase reversal
- Generator run
- Generator fault
- Stair doors unlocked
- Smoke control system in operation

Controls are switches that control features external to the fire alarm system.

Examples of Control Switches:
- Remote fire pump start
- Remote generator start
- Smoke control manual switches
- Stair unlocking switches

Considerations – Zoning and Annunciation
- Provide separate panel for each building served.
- Locate for rapid fire department access near the primary entrance or in the fire command center.
- Include basic information: Floor, zone, device type (alarm or supervisory).
- Meet zone size limitations.
- Arrange devices subject to unwanted alarms as supervisory.
- Indicate area covered by sprinkler systems, not location of switches.
- Include status indicators for power and external devices.
- Include control switches for other fire protection features.

GRAPHIC DISPLAYS

If an annunciator shows any location-related information that is not obvious, a graphic diagram should be provided. Examples are zone boundaries, room names, or room numbers. Diagrams enable firefighters to determine where to investigate alarms originating in locations with designations such as "Zone 2 East, " "Suite 121, " or "Main Electric Room. "

The graphic display may be a separate, printed diagram mounted on the wall adjacent to the annunciator. Or, it may be integrated with the annunciator, in which case it is called a "graphic annunciator. " Some jurisdictions may require graphic annunciators.

The design of the diagram is very important in enabling firefighters to rapidly obtain needed information. Fire departments may have regulations or policies outlining their requirements or preferences. Some code officials require annunciators throughout their jurisdiction to have standardized features.

Orientation of the diagram will be important in aiding firefighters to visually process the information it contains. The farthest point of the building beyond the annunciator's location should be at the top of the diagram.

Designers should begin with the building's outline in creating diagrams. Zones would be identified by the boundary lines between them. Likewise, for alarms designated by room, suite, or tenant, these locations should be shown. A "You Are Here" indicator shows the viewers where they are in the building.

NFPA 13 permits most sprinkler zones to cover as much as 52,000 square feet. Therefore, multiple alarm zones may cover one sprinkler zone. If there is one sprinkler zone on a floor and multiple alarm zones, lamp or LED annunciators should report only the floor and device type. An alarm from another device type will light the appropriate zone lamp. If there are multiple sprinkler zones per floor, and sprinkler and alarm zone boundaries are not coordinated, separate diagrams can show each.

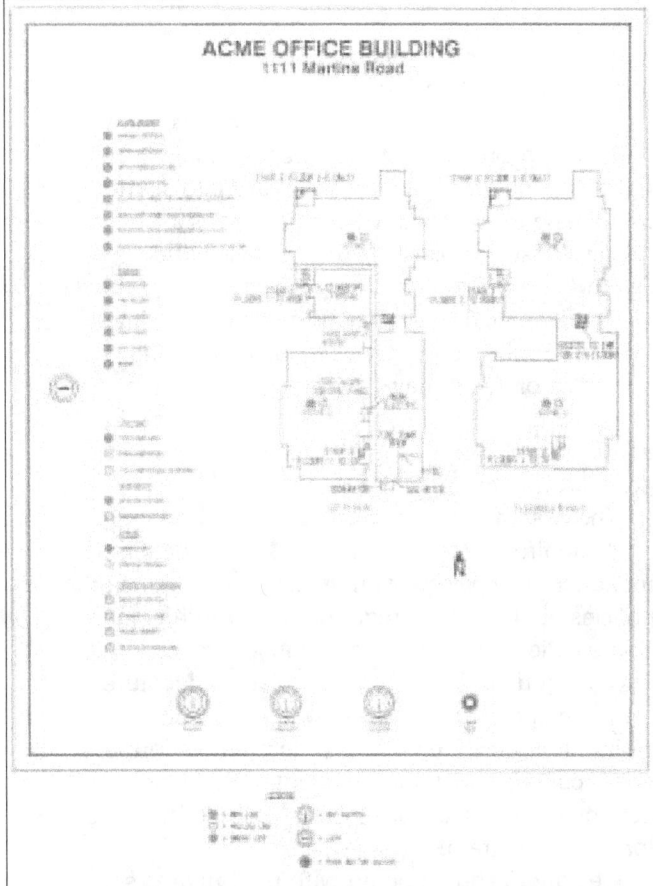

ACME OFFICE BUILDING
1111 Marlins Road

(Fig. 6.4) Good diagram, with clearly organized and labeled lamps, as well as building features to assist the fire service.

Consistent designations for any floor indications used in the building will avoid confusion. For example, it is imperative that floor designations on the signs mounted in stairways, elevator cars, and elevator lobbies, be consistent with the annunciator so the firefighters report to the correct floor.

In addition to information about floors, zones, and devices, many features of the building could be shown on the diagram. These include fire protection systems and building components that the fire department needs to be aware of (Figure 6.4).

Designers should remember that modifications to the building or its layout may require changes to the diagram. An annunciator with inaccurate information could be worse than no annunciator at all.

Considerations – Graphic Displays

- Include graphics to show location-related information.
- Include standard features required for the jurisdiction.
- Coordinate the orientation of the diagram with its location in the building.
- Provide separate sprinkler diagrams if zone boundaries do not coincide with other alarm devices.
- Coordinate floor level designations with elevators and stairways.
- Include the following building features:
  o Building address;
  o North direction arrow;
  o Stairs, their identification, and the floors they serve;
  o Elevators, their identification, and the floors they serve;
  o Elevator machine rooms;
  o Exterior entrances;
  o Standpipe locations;
  o Location of utility controls (electric, gas, fuel);
  o Fire alarm control panel;
  o Fire pump(s);
  o Fire department connection(s).

OSHA
Occupational Safety and
Health Administration

FIRE DEPARTMENT NOTIFICATION

Building or fire codes often require fire alarm systems to automatically alert the responsible fire brigade, fire department, or other emergency response forces. The important consideration for fire department response is reporting the correct location. Often an alarm service or off-site location will receive the alarm signal and then retransmit it to the fire department and/or fire brigade.

It is crucial that the address reported to the fire department match the address where the alarm originated. If a building has multiple addresses, the one with the fire alarm annunciator or fire command center, should be reported. If a building includes separate, independent annunciators, coordinate the remote signal with the correct annunciator location (Figure 6.5).

Larger buildings with multiple sections or multiple entrances can be confusing. If possible, remote fire department notification should include information on the section, wing, or entrance where units should report, so firefighters may investigate an alarm originating from the corresponding area. In addition, strobe lights at entrances corresponding to the alarm location for on-site notification can greatly assist the fire department (Figure 6.6).

(Fig. 6.5) One of two annunciators in a building with four wings, which fronts on three different streets.

(Fig. 6.6) Strobes above each tenant entry door indicate the tenant where an alarm originates in this building, which has multiple tenants with different addresses fronting on two streets.

Considerations - Fire Department Notification
- Report the correct location/address.
- Report the entrance with the alarm annunciator or fire command center.
- Report the section or wing of the building, if available.
- Report device type, if possible.

VOICE ALARM SYSTEMS

Voice alarms automatically send a voice evacuation message to speakers in selected areas of high-rises or expansive buildings, hospitals, and other buildings where total evacuation is impractical. A typical high-rise arrangement would provide for the following areas to automatically receive a pre-recorded evacuation signal: the floor where the alarm originates and the floors above and below it. Arriving firefighters can evacuate additional areas by manually activating one, multiple, or all floors with the manual select switches in the command center. They also can override the pre-recorded message and broadcast live voice announcements to any or all evacuation zones with a microphone at the command center. Adjacent to each manual select switch, visual indicators show which evacuation zones are activated at any given time (Figure 6.7).

Arrangement of evacuation zones depends upon the design of the building and any evacuation plan in place. Each floor is typically one evacuation zone. Areas that are not separated by fire or smoke barriers should not be divided into multiple evacuation zones. However, if a floor is divided by fire or smoke barriers to enable occupants to take refuge on either side, multiple evacuation zones should be provided. Operators at the command center will only be able to give different instructions to those on either side of the barriers if the zone boundaries coincide with the rated barriers.

In addition to normally occupied spaces, most building and fire codes require speakers in stairways and elevator cabs. Each stairway and each bank of elevators should comprise a single evacuation zone. In a building with selective evacuation, it is undesirable to automatically activate the speakers in these areas. Also, there are typically no detectors to warn of fire or smoke within the stairways or elevator cabs. Each of these zones typically has "manual-only" selection capability for the operators in the fire command center. If a stairway has detectors, the speakers in that particular stairway could be configured into a separate, automatically activated evacuation zone. Designers should ensure that evacuation signals are not heard in areas that are not to be evacuated.

(Fig. 6.7) The grey panel is a voice alarm panel. The lower window shows the microphone and the manual select switches for the different evacuation zones.

OSHA
Occupational Safety and
Health Administration

Floors that are physically open to one another should be arranged as a single evacuation zone. This avoids the confusion possible when occupants in portions of the space hear an evacuation signal, but cannot clearly decipher it. A common example of this situation is a series of parking garage levels connected by open ramps. The group of interconnected levels should be designed as a single evacuation zone on the "floor, floor above, and floor below" automatic evacuation scenario.

Atriums and other large open spaces spanning multiple floors also deserve special attention in buildings with selective evacuation. The arrangement depends upon the egress arrangement and the building's evacuation plan. The entire atrium should comprise one evacuation zone. It may be desirable to activate only the atrium zone upon receipt of an alarm signal from within the atrium, and not from alarm signals in other areas. Designers should consider the legibility of signals in areas adjacent to the atrium, so as not to cause occupant confusion.

Considerations - Voice Alarm Systems

- Arrange evacuation zone boundaries along fire or smoke separations.
- Coordinate the evacuation zones with the building evacuation plan.
- Place areas or floors open to one another in a single zone.
- Arrange each bank of elevators into a manual-select zone.
- Arrange each stairway into a separate zone (manual-select type if no initiating devices within stairway).
- Arrange each atrium on a separate zone, and consider message legibility when arranging activation of adjacent areas.

FIRE DEPARTMENT COMMUNICATIONS SYSTEMS

Fire department communications systems are two-way telephone systems typically required in high-rise buildings. The command center contains the control unit with the main handset for use by the fire department commanders (Figure 6.8a). Either handsets or jacks for handsets are then placed in areas of the building for firefighters to communicate with the command center (Figure 6.8b). If the system uses jacks, a number of portable handsets with plugs are provided in the command center for distribution to firefighters.

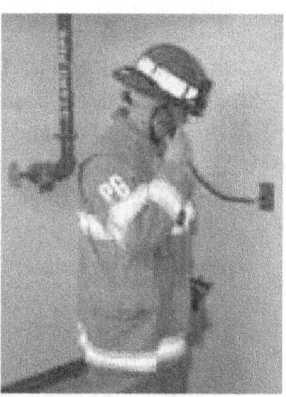

(Fig. 6.8a) Fire officer speaking into the handset at the control panel for a fire department communication system. This panel also houses the handsets used by firefighters at remote jacks.

(Fig. 6.8b) A firefighter using a handset in a remote jack located inside a stairway.

Designers should plan for handsets or jacks in locations where firefighters are likely to be operating. NFPA 72 requires only one handset or jack per floor, one per exit stairway, and one in each fire pump room. NFPA 101 requires them on every level in each enclosed stairway, each elevator car, and each elevator lobby. The IBC currently requires handsets or jacks in the same locations as NFPA 101 and also in standby power rooms, fire pump rooms, and areas of refuge. These additional jacks or handsets can provide more rapid communications from these critical areas.

Both the IBC and NFPA 101 contain exceptions that allow fire departments to approve their radio systems as a substitute for two-way telephone systems. For a radio system to be equivalent, the radio signals should be operable in the same areas (the command center and each remote jack or handset location). To exercise this option, designers or building owners should test radio signals and document of successful results. Signal retransmission devices may be necessary; this is discussed further in the section, Firefighter Radio Signal Retransmission Systems, on page 61.

Considerations - Fire Department Communications Systems
- Locate control panel in fire command center.
- Locate jacks or handsets in stairs, elevator cars, elevator lobbies, standby power rooms, fire pump rooms, and areas of refuge.
- When a fire department is willing to allow its radio system to substitute, specify a signal transmission analysis and retransmission devices, if required.

(Fig. 6.9) Fire command center next to main entrance. The sign on the room should be visible to responding firefighters.

FIRE COMMAND CENTERS

Building or fire codes typically require high-rise buildings to have a dedicated room or other location containing fire alarm and related fire protection control equipment. These are called "Fire Command Centers" in NFPA 72 and in the IBC. The term "Central Control Station" is used in NFPA 101 and NFPA 5000. Yet another term, "Emergency Command Center," is used in NFPA 1. Industry also uses the expression "Fire Control Room."

Both the IBC and NFPA 72 require the room containing the fire command center to be one-hour fire-rated. These rooms often have exterior entrances which should be prominently marked (Figure 6.9). NFPA 72 and NFPA 101 permit lobbies or other approved locations instead of a dedicated, fire-rated room. The IBC requires the room to be at least 96 square feet, with a minimum dimension of 8 feet. NFPA 72 requires at least a three-foot clearance in front of all control equipment.

The IBC contains a comprehensive list of equipment required in a fire command center. The lists in NFPA 1, NFPA 101 and NFPA 5000 are about half as long, and all of these items are on the list in the IBC as well. The additional items in the IBC may greatly assist firefighters in their operations. These include: a work table, building plans, fire protection system plans, and controls for air handling equipment, smoke control systems, and the generator (Figure 6.10).

If a building has multiple fire command centers, visual indicators should show, at a glance, which fire command center is in control at any given time.

(Fig. 6.10) Fire command center with fire alarm and communications equipment, a work table, and adequate work space for the incident command staff.

Considerations - Fire Command Centers
- Use a dedicated room unless the local fire department permits and sanctions another location.
- Include all fire protection control panels and supporting equipment.
- Provide visual cross-reference indicators for multiple command centers.

OSHA
Occupational Safety and
Health Administration

Chapter 7
Other Systems

FIREFIGHTER EMERGENCY POWER SYSTEMS

Firefighters regularly use electric power for lights, ventilation fans, or other tools. In large or tall buildings they must run extensive lengths of electric cable to feed equipment in remote areas of the building. A fixed, emergency power system built into the building can substitute for these long cable runs, and save time and effort. This is analogous to standpipe systems substituting for long hose lays. In fact, one approach is to require an emergency power system whenever standpipes are required.

Emergency power systems include one or more dedicated electric circuits feeding a series of electrical receptacles (Figure 7.1). They are wired on an emergency circuit in the building and connected to any backup power sources in the building. In this manner, the outlets are continuously available for fire department use, even after the main power is shut down.

The designer should find out first if a jurisdiction requires a firefighter emergency power system and what specific criteria must be met. The plug type the fire department uses for its electrical equipment (Figure 7.2) determines the receptacle type. The

(Fig. 7.2) A weather-resistant receptacle cover opened, showing the twist-lock receptacle.

wiring methods and over-current protection must meet 29 CFR Subpart S and any other local or state codes.

Receptacles may be located on every level inside each enclosed stairway. Some jurisdictions may require, or prefer, them to be located outside the stairwell. Additional receptacles may be placed to accommodate a maximum length of cable. Or, simply locating one receptacle next to each standpipe fire hose connection (Figure 7.1) may provide good distribution.

Mark receptacles so that firefighters can spot them easily. For example, the designer could specify that each be painted red and labeled "For Fire Department Use Only."

(Fig. 7.1) Firefighter emergency power receptacle next to a standpipe fire hose connection inside of a stair enclosure.

Considerations - Firefighter Emergency Power Systems
- Specify installation when required or desired.
- Specify the appropriate circuitry and receptacle type.
- Specify connection to any standby power sources in the building.
- Provide receptacles in convenient, accessible locations.
- Mark receptacles appropriately.

FIREFIGHTER BREATHING AIR SYSTEMS

Firefighters use self-contained breathing apparatus (SCBA) for interior fire fighting. SCBA air is supplied by cylinders (often referred to as "bottles") that have a limited amount of air. When depleted, these air cylinders need to be refilled or replaced with full ones. Some fire service organizations have specialized vehicles that contain systems known as "cascade systems" that refill breathing air cylinders at fire scenes.

A firefighter breathing air system is a system of piping within a tall building or a sprawling structure that enables firefighters to refill their breathing apparatus cylinders at remote interior locations. These systems are essentially air standpipe systems. A few jurisdictions in the U.S. require such systems for high-rise buildings, or for long (i.e., over 300 feet) underground tunnels (both pedestrian and transportation).

Without such systems, firefighters must carry additional breathing air cylinders to a staging area, and others must transport cylinders back and forth from a supply point outside. Permanently installed breathing air systems make emergency operations safer and more efficient by eliminating the need to carry extra cylinders, reducing the time and personnel needed for logistical support. However, proper function is dependent upon careful, thorough design, as well as regular maintenance.

A firefighter breathing air system consists of a piping distribution system that runs from a supply point to interior "fill stations" or "fill panels." Fill panels contain short sections of hose with connections that fit firefighter's air cylinders. Fill stations are larger enclosures in which cylinders are replenished within a blast fragmentation container using rigid fill connections. Both alternatives have the necessary valves, gauges, regulators, and locks to prevent tampering. Their mounting height should facilitate easy connection of cylinders.

A good location for fill points (panels or stations) is just outside enclosed, fire-rated stairs. Placement at every second or third level provides reasonable coverage. This distribution enables firefighters to locate fill points quickly and set up a replenishment operation in safe proximity to the fire. With fill points just outside the stairs, refill operations will not impede stairway traffic (whether firefighters or occupants). A sign within the stair

enclosure, at each level with fill points, can indicate the location of fill points (for example: "Breathing Air Fill Panel, Out Door and 10 Feet to the Right."). Fill points should only be located inside the stair enclosure after careful consideration by the fire department and if additional space is allocated for refilling operations. For tunnels, designers should locate fill points a reasonable spacing apart, perhaps 200 feet.

The supply to the distribution system will vary according to fire department capabilities and preferences. One approach is to provide one or more exterior fire department connection panels through which the fire department supplies air from a mobile air supply unit. Another is to provide fixed air storage cylinders within the building, and an exterior backup fill connection. The fixed storage components would be in a lockable, air conditioned, fire-rated room with emergency lighting and a pressure relief vent.

All fire department fill connection panels should be in weather-resistant, locked enclosures marked to indicate their use. Many of the design considerations for these connections are similar to those in Chapter 5 for sprinkler/standpipe connections. They should be located to make it possible for the fill lines on the air fill unit to reach the connection panel.

The designer should provide a fire lane or a road for the mobile air fill unit to access each fill connection. Some of the design considerations in the section, Fire Apparatus Access, on page 11, also apply, in particular the paragraphs on material, gates, barricades, security measures, and marking. The clear height and width would need to accommodate only the fill unit, unless it also serves as access for larger fire apparatus.

Reliability features are highly desirable on breathing air systems. The piping should stay pressurized and the system should include a low air pressure monitoring device. Air quality may be supervised with carbon monoxide and moisture monitors. The designer should specify an air quality analysis for the initial system acceptance as well as ongoing periodic testing. The designer should call for good installation practices, including keeping the piping free of oils, dirt, construction materials, or other contaminants.

OSHA
Occupational Safety and
Health Administration

For adequate protection throughout an incident, all components of the system should be separated from other portions of the building or tunnel by fire-rated construction. A rating equivalent to that required for stair enclosures is reasonable.

The performance of the entire system should be specified in terms of the number of air cylinders to be filled simultaneously at remote locations, the fill pressure, and the fill time. This will dictate the size of the distribution piping and any air storage cylinders. All components should be specified for use with breathing air, and marked to indicate their use.

Considerations - Firefighter Breathing Air Systems

- Obtain and follow all applicable laws and regulations.
- Specify lockable fill stations or fill panels.
- Specify proper mounting height for fill panels or fill stations.
- Locate fill stations or fill panels just outside stairways.
- Provide signage in stairs at levels of fill panels/fill stations.
- Specify on-site air storage when required.
- Specify weatherproof lockable fire department connection panel(s).
- Locate exterior fire department connection panel(s) near access for the mobile air unit.
- Locate multiple exterior fire department connection panels remote from each other.
- Specify piping and other components suitable for high pressure breathing air.
- Specify that all components be marked for their use.
- Specify CO monitor and low air pressure alarm.
- Specify system performance as follows:
  o Minimum number of cylinders to be simultaneously filled;
  o Maximum cylinder pressure;
  o Maximum fill time.
- Specify air quality analysis at acceptance, and periodic testing.

FIREFIGHTER RADIO SIGNAL RETRANSMISSION SYSTEMS

Fire department portable radios are frequently unreliable inside buildings and other structures such as tunnels. Construction materials, earth, and changes in the radio frequency environment can greatly reduce the strength of radio signals. If a firefighter inside is unable to transmit or receive, he or she must relocate closer to an exterior opening, move to a different floor, use an alternate means of communication, or resort to runners or direct voice communications. Cell phone signals are affected by the same factors as radio signals. Land line phones will allow firefighters to communicate with dispatchers, but not other units; they may also be affected by the incident occurring in the building. All of these factors may delay operations, and create greater challenges in maintaining crew integrity (Figure 7.3).

New technology can improve signal transmission within buildings and structures through fixed communications infrastructures. Passive approaches simply provide a conduit to assist in the transmission of signals. However, active methods involve powered devices to amplify and retransmit signals.

For example, the "passive antenna system" includes both an internal and an external antenna, connected with a short coaxial cable. A "radiating cable," also known as a "leaky coax" is a network of coaxial cables with slots in the outer conductor that create a continuous antenna effect.

Increasing in popularity is an active signal transmission method involving a signal booster also known as a "Bi-Directional Amplifier," or simply BDA. These powered devices amplify signals between an external antenna and one or more internal antennae. Both reception and transmission are amplified messages on portable radios within the building. A network of antennae placed at strategic locations or a leaky coaxial cable distribute signals throughout the coverage area.

Some installations combine passive and active approaches. Passive antennae generally work well in small, well-defined areas. BDAs function well in larger, diverse areas that need a coverage solution.

Some jurisdictions have adopted laws or ordinances concerning public safety radio communications. In others, designers should consider specifying a study to determine the possible need for retransmission devices. Installing stationary communications infrastructures in high-rise buildings and tunnels is one way to resolve communication problems like those encountered by the Fire Department of New York on September 11, 2001.

Without laws requiring this equipment, cost considerations may discourage owners from voluntary installations. However, owners of high-rises or other target hazards may be swayed by increases in property value or improved safety for tenants. Alternatively, in high-rise buildings where firefighter communication systems are required, a code official may permit the substitution of fixed communications infrastructures as discussed in the section, Fire Department Communications Systems, on page 57. Perhaps, in the future, insurance companies will offer lower premiums for buildings containing such installations.

Many local communications ordinances currently in effect in the U.S. contain specific requirements for system performance. These include signal strength, area coverage, reliability, secondary power supply, interference filters, acceptance testing upon completion, and ongoing periodic testing.

(Fig. 7.3) Chief Officer on portable radio.

Considerations - Firefighter Radio Communications
- Follow any local laws or ordinances for fixed communications infrastructures.
- Investigate the feasibility of voluntary compliance in other jurisdictions.
- Specify minimum signal strength.
- Specify percentage of the building to meet the signal strength.
- Specify the percentage of time that signal strength is to be available.
- Specify secondary power for at least 12 hours of continuous, full-load operation.
- Specify filters needed to block interference from nearby channels.
- Specify a suitable acceptance test of all system functions and features.

SMOKE CONTROL SYSTEMS

Smoke control systems (or smoke management systems) are mechanical systems that control the movement of smoke during a fire. Most are intended to protect occupants while they are evacuating or being sheltered in place. The most common systems referenced in current codes are atrium smoke exhaust systems and stair-pressurization systems. In some specialized cases, zoned smoke control systems may be provided. These feature zones or floors that are either pressurized or exhausted to keep smoke from spreading.

The IBC contains mandatory provisions for smoke control systems. Designers can find NFPA's detailed provisions in two non-mandatory documents, the Recommended Practice for Smoke Control Systems (NFPA 92A) and the Guide for Smoke Management Systems in Malls, Atria, and Large Areas (NFPA 92B).

The manual controls required or provided for smoke control systems are a primary consideration for the fire service. These manual controls can override automatic controls that activate these systems. When fire department personnel arrive, they can assess whether the automatic modes are functioning as intended. Incident commanders may then use the manual controls to select a different mode or turn any given zone off. It is imperative that these controls override any other manual or automatic controls at any other location.

A simple, straightforward control panel with manual switches for the smoke control system(s) will assist a firefighter who may be trying to decipher how the controls work just after awakening in the middle of the night. Also, similar to annunciators, the fire department may have specific requirements or recommendations, and may prefer uniformity of panels within their jurisdiction.

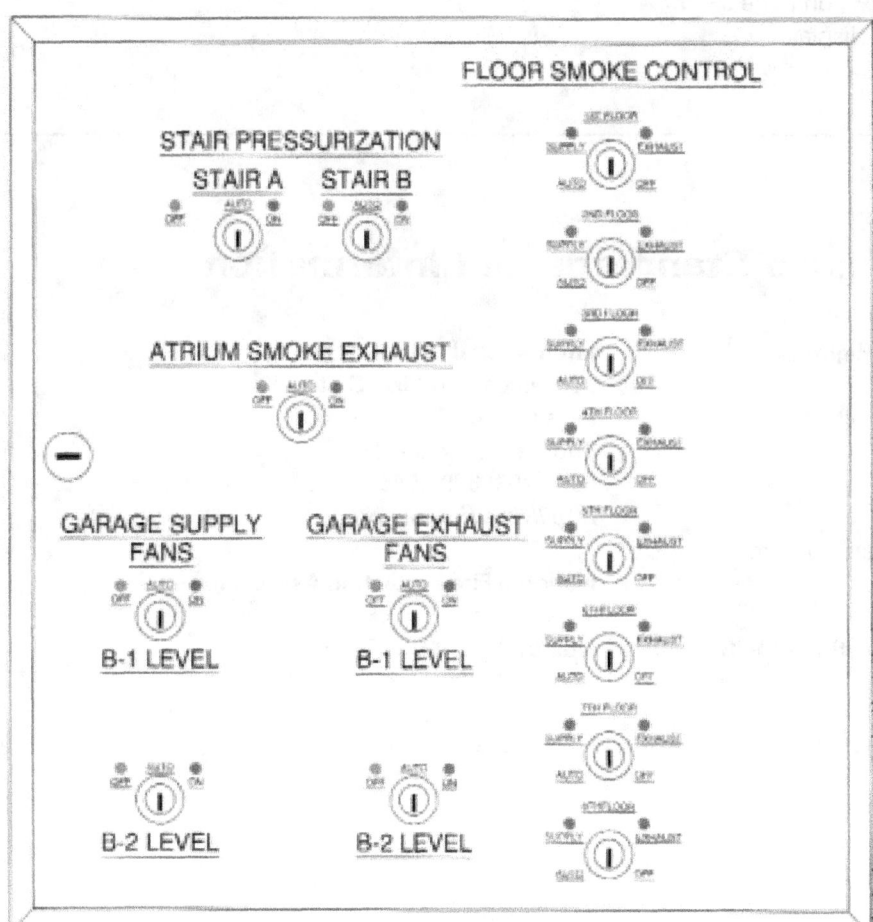

(Fig. 7.4) A well-designed, easy-to-understand diagram of a smoke control panel. Each system has a single, clearly labeled switch to select each mode.

Both the IBC and NFPA 92A call for status indicators for each fan, damper, and other device. The ICC requires individual controls for each of these devices, but permits them to be combined for complex systems. A system need not be very large to be considered complex.

A good, simple panel layout might feature a single switch for each system or zone (Figure 7.4). Each different position of the switch places the system in a given mode, and the corresponding activation or setting of the individual devices would be configured "behind the scenes." For example, a stair pressurization system might contain a three-position switch for each of three modes: "automatic," "pressurize," and "off."

Zoned smoke control systems are often arranged with each floor as a separate zone. In other cases, a floor may be split into multiple zones. These should be indicated on a graphic display, either on or adjacent to the smoke control panel. See the section, Graphic Displays, on page 53, for additional guidance on graphic displays.

Designers should not confuse smoke control systems with smoke or heat venting systems. The latter are mechanical systems for the removal of smoke. They are often arranged to activate only manually. In some cases, they only remove smoke after an incident.

Considerations – Smoke Control Systems
- Settings for atrium smoke exhaust switches: "auto," "exhaust," "off."
- Settings for stair pressurization switches: "auto," "pressurize," "off."
- Settings for zoned smoke control switches: "auto," "exhaust," "pressurize," "off."
- If there is more than one zone per floor, provide a graphic diagram.
- Settings for manual smoke venting system switches: "exhaust," "off."

Appendix

Sources of Referenced Standards and Information

American Association of State Highway and Transportation Officials
444 North Capitol Street, NW, Suite 249
Washington, DC 20001
Phone: (202) 624-5800
Fax: (202) 624-5806
http://www.transportation.org/aashto/home.nsf/FrontPage

American National Standards Institute (ANSI)
1819 L Street, NW, 6th floor
Washington, DC 20036
Phone: (202) 293-8020
Fax: (202) 293-9287
http://www.ansi.org

American Water Works Association
6666 W. Quincy Ave.
Denver, CO 80235
Phone: (303) 794-7711 or (800) 926-7337
Fax: (303) 347-0804
http://www.awwa.org

International Code Council
5203 Leesburg Pike, Suite 600
Falls Church, VA 22041
Phone: (888) 422-7233
Fax: (703) 379-1546
http://www.iccsafe.org

National Fire Protection Association
1 Batterymarch Park
Quincy, MA 02169-7471
Phone: (800) 344-3555
Fax: (800) 593-6372
http://www.nfpa.org

OSHA Assistance

OSHA can provide extensive help through a variety of programs, including technical assistance about effective safety and health programs, state plans, workplace consultations, voluntary protection programs, strategic partnerships, training and education, and more. An overall commitment to workplace safety and health can add value to your business, to your workplace and to your life.

Safety and Health Program Management Guidelines

Effective management of worker safety and health protection is a decisive factor in reducing the extent and severity of work-related injuries and illnesses and their related costs. In fact, an effective safety and health program forms the basis of good worker protection and can save time and money (about $4 for every dollar spent) and increase productivity and reduce worker injuries, illnesses and related workers' compensation costs.

To assist employers and employees in developing effective safety and health programs, OSHA published recommended *Safety and Health Program Management Guidelines* (54 *Federal Register* (16): 3904-3916, January 26, 1989). These voluntary guidelines apply to all places of employment covered by OSHA.

The guidelines identify four general elements critical to the development of a successful safety and health management program:

- Management leadership and employee involvement.
- Work analysis.
- Hazard prevention and control.
- Safety and health training.

The guidelines recommend specific actions, under each of these general elements, to achieve an effective safety and health program. The *Federal Register* notice is available online at www.osha.gov

State Programs

The Occupational Safety and Health Act of 1970 (*OSH Act*) encourages states to develop and operate their own job safety and health plans. OSHA approves and monitors these plans. Twenty-four states, Puerto Rico and the Virgin Islands currently operate approved state plans: 22 cover both private and public (state and local government) employment; the Connecticut, New Jersey, New York and Virgin Islands plans cover the public sector only. States and territories with their own OSHA-approved occupational safety and health plans must adopt standards identical to, or at least as effective as, the Federal standards.

Consultation Services

Consultation assistance is available on request to employers who want help in establishing and maintaining a safe and healthful workplace. Largely funded by OSHA, the service is provided at no cost to the employer. Primarily developed for smaller employers with more hazardous operations, the consultation service is delivered by state governments employing professional safety and health consultants. Comprehensive assistance includes an appraisal of all mechanical systems, work practices and occupational safety and health hazards of the workplace and all aspects of the employer's present job safety and health program. In addition, the service offers assistance to employers in developing and implementing an effective safety and health program. No penalties are proposed or citations issued for hazards identified by the consultant. OSHA provides consultation assistance to the employer with the assurance that his or her name and firm and any information about the workplace will not be routinely reported to OSHA enforcement staff.

Under the consultation program, certain exemplary employers may request participation in OSHA's Safety and Health Achievement Recognition Program (SHARP). Eligibility for participation in SHARP includes receiving a comprehensive consultation visit, demonstrating exemplary achievements in workplace safety and health by abating all identified hazards and developing an excellent safety and health program.

Employers accepted into SHARP may receive an exemption from programmed inspections (not complaint or accident investigation inspections) for a period of one year. For more information concerning consultation assistance, see the OSHA website at www.osha.gov

Voluntary Protection Programs (VPP)

Voluntary Protection Programs and on-site consultation services, when coupled with an effective enforcement program, expand worker protection to help meet the goals of the *OSH Act*. The three levels of VPP are Star, Merit, and Demonstration designed to recognize outstanding achievements by companies that have successfully incorporated comprehensive safety and health programs into their total management system. The VPPs motivate others to achieve excellent safety and health results in the same outstanding way as they establish a cooperative relationship between employers, employees and OSHA.

For additional information on VPP and how to apply, contact the OSHA regional offices listed at the end of this publication.

Strategic Partnership Program

OSHA's Strategic Partnership Program, the newest member of OSHA's cooperative programs, helps encourage, assist and recognize the efforts of partners to eliminate serious workplace hazards and achieve a high level of worker safety and health. Whereas OSHA's Consultation Program and VPP entail one-on-one relationships between OSHA and individual worksites, most strategic partnerships seek to have a broader impact by building cooperative relationships with groups of employers and employees. These partnerships are voluntary, cooperative relationships between OSHA, employers, employee representatives and others (e.g., trade unions, trade and professional associations, universities and other government agencies).

For more information on this and other cooperative programs, contact your nearest OSHA office, or visit OSHA's website at www.osha.gov

Alliance Programs

The Alliances Program enables organizations committed to workplace safety and health to collaborate with OSHA to prevent injuries and illnesses in the workplace. OSHA and the Alliance participants work together to reach out to, educate and lead the nation's employers and their employees in improving and advancing workplace safety and health.

Groups that can form an Alliance with OSHA include employers, labor unions, trade or professional groups, educational institutions and government agencies. In some cases, organizations may be building on existing relationships with OSHA that were developed through other cooperative programs.

There are few formal program requirements for Alliances and the agreements do not include an enforcement component. However, OSHA and the participating organizations must define, implement and meet a set of short- and long-term goals that fall into three categories: training and education; outreach and communication; and promoting the national dialogue on workplace safety and health.

OSHA Training and Education

OSHA area offices offer a variety of information services, such as compliance assistance, technical advice, publications, audiovisual aids and speakers for special engagements. OSHA's Training Institute in Arlington Heights, IL, provides basic and advanced courses in safety and health for Federal and state compliance officers, state consultants, Federal agency personnel, and private sector employers, employees and their representatives.

The OSHA Training Institute also has established OSHA Training Institute Education Centers to address the increased demand for its courses from the private sector and from other Federal agencies. These centers are nonprofit colleges, universities and other organizations that have been selected after a competition for participation in the program.

OSHA also provides funds to nonprofit organizations, through grants, to conduct workplace training and education in subjects where OSHA believes there is a lack of workplace training. Grants are awarded annually. Grant recipients are expected to contribute 20 percent of the total grant cost.

For more information on grants, training and education, contact the OSHA Training Institute, Office of Training and Education, 2020 South Arlington Heights Road, Arlington Heights, IL 60005, (847) 297-4810 or see "Outreach" on OSHA's website at www.osha.gov. For further information on any OSHA program, contact your nearest OSHA area or regional office listed at the end of this publication.

Information Available Electronically

OSHA has a variety of materials and tools available on its website at www.osha.gov. These include *e-Tools* such as *Expert Advisors, Electronic Compliance Assistance Tools (e-cats), Technical Links*; regulations, directives and publications; videos and other information for employers and employees. OSHA's software programs and compliance assistance tools walk you through challenging safety and health issues and common problems to find the best solutions for your workplace.

A wide variety of OSHA materials, including standards, interpretations, directives, and more, can be purchased on CD-ROM from the U.S. Government Printing Office, Superintendent of Documents, phone toll-free (866) 512-1800.

OSHA
Occupational Safety and
Health Administration

OSHA Regional Offices

Region I
(CT,* ME, MA, NH, RI, VT*)
JFK Federal Building, Room E340
Boston, MA 02203
(617) 565-9860

Region II
(NJ,* NY,* PR,* VI*)
201 Varick Street, Room 670
New York, NY 10014
(212) 337-2378

Region III
(DE, DC, MD,* PA, VA,* WV)
The Curtis Center
170 S. Independence Mall West
Suite 740 West
Philadelphia, PA 19106-3309
(215) 861-4900

Region IV
(AL, FL, GA, KY,* MS, NC,* SC,* TN*)
61 Forsyth Street, SW
Atlanta, GA 30303
(404) 562-2300

Region V
(IL, IN,* MI,* MN,* OH, WI)
230 South Dearborn Street
Room 3244
Chicago, IL 60604
(312) 353-2220

Region VI
(AR, LA, NM,* OK, TX)
525 Griffin Street, Room 602
Dallas, TX 75202
(214) 767-4731 or 4736 x224

Region VII
(IA,* KS, MO, NE)
City Center Square
1100 Main Street, Suite 800
Kansas City, MO 64105
(816) 426-5861

Region VIII
(CO, MT, ND, SD, UT,* WY*)
1999 Broadway, Suite 1690
PO Box 46550
Denver, CO 80202-5716
(720) 264-6550

Region IX
(American Samoa, AZ,* CA,* HI,* NV,*
Northern Mariana Islands)
71 Stevenson Street, Room 420
San Francisco, CA 94105
(415) 975-4310

Region X
(AK,* ID, OR,* WA*)
1111 Third Avenue, Suite 715
Seattle, WA 98101-3212
(206) 553-5930

   * These states and territories operate their own OSHA-approved job safety and health programs and cover state and local government workers as well as private sector workers. The Connecticut, New Jersey, New York and Virgin Islands plans cover public employees only. States with approved programs must have standards that are identical to, or at least as effective as, the Federal standards.

   Note: To get contact information for OSHA Area Offices, OSHA-approved State Plans and OSHA Consultation Projects, please visit us online at www.osha.gov or call us at 1-800-321-OSHA.